MARRIAGE TAKES MORE THAN

MARRIAGE TAKES
MORE THAN

Bill and Anabel Gillham

Wolgemuth & Hyatt, Publishers, Inc.
Brentwood, Tennessee

The mission of Wolgemuth & Hyatt, Publishers, Inc. is to publish and distribute books that lead individuals toward:

- A personal faith in the one true God: Father, Son, and Holy Spirit;

- A lifestyle of practical discipleship; and

- A worldview that is consistent with the historic, Christian faith.

Moreover, the Company endeavors to accomplish this mission at a reasonable profit and in a manner which glorifies God and serves His Kingdom.

Wolgemuth & Hyatt, Publishers, Inc.
P.O. Box 1941, Brentwood, Tennessee 37027.
Printed in the United States of America.

Library of Congress Cataloging-in-Publication Data

Gillham, Bill.
Marriage takes more than two / Bill and Anabel Gillham.
    p.   cm.
ISBN 0-943497-42-6
1. Marriage — religious aspects — Christianity. I. Gillham, Anabel. II. Title.

BV835.G544   1989
248.4 — dc20   89-5726
                                                        CIP

To the Marriage Maker,
the Essence of Our Oneness

CONTENTS

ACKNOWLEDGMENTS

We give our thanks to those God has called to be an integral part of our ministry as encouragers, supporters, and dear brothers and sisters. Because you have loved us and shared your lives with us, we have grown in our capacity for understanding, for compassion, and for consecration to persevere in the role God has given to us.

We would like to give a special word of thanks to our son, Will Gillham, whose editing proved invaluable.

FOREWORD

The best way to experience the insight, humor, and very valuable ministry of Bill and Anabel Gillham is to know them and experience their lives firsthand. Thousands of others have watched and listened as they have worked their magic in conferences, churches, and seminars. Most will not have even that opportunity, and so tapes and books will have to suffice. Jamie and I have benefited greatly from our friendship with Bill and Anabel through the years. Now you can do the same by enjoying this extremely practical book on Christian marriage.

Three important elements converge in this book, making it unique. The first and foremost quality of the Gillham's ministry is a belief that Biblical instruction is not only for salvation of our souls but is also for our lives as well. Each individual partner in a marriage is first a unique creation of God, and since He made us, He alone can fix us and make us able to function as whole people in a marriage. In short, this book takes good theology and good psychology seriously, because both the Bible and our personalities are creations of God.

The second element of this book is the long experience that Bill and Anabel have had with actual people in real marriages. So very much of what we believe about normalcy in marriage today has been gained through media. Here the situations often are not the creations of real life or of God but are the arbitrary concoctions of a novelist or playwright playing God, often weaving into the characters their own personal struggles, wishful thinking, angers, responses, and a host of social theory not yet accepted by most of society.

Bill and Anabel deal daily with real people who have built into their lives the values, presuppositions, struggles, and needs that are their own and therefore must be dealt with by a kind of return to the basics. And for the Christian that means: How does my behavior mesh with God's will and the role he gave me in the world? At the root, this book argues for faith that expresses itself in submission to the creative wisdom of our Creator, who thought up the whole idea of male and female, sexuality, marriage, children, family, and human diversity.

Finally, there is the truly empathetic tone that comes through as two very different people, Bill and Anabel, with disarming transparency give us an intimate look into their personal growth process and the practical lessons that have helped them through their daily challenges. They do not suggest a state of bliss where no problems exist but more realistically help us see the source of our pain and then present us with ways that we can will and act to solve our conflicts and struggles.

As I read this manuscript, I kept saying to myself, *I want my own kids to read this—this book will help any marriage.*

Jay Kesler
Upland, Indiana

To Understand This Book,
You Must Read the . . .

INTRODUCTION

There must be thousands of good books and seminars on improving your marriage, so why should
Anabel and I write another one? Surely there's no dramatic *new* discovery which will turn a sour marriage into
a sweet one and a good one into a great one! We believe
there is. It is as old as the New Testament, but to the
Christian who has not understood, it will seem new; it is
the "mystery" of which Paul wrote in his letter to the
Colossians (see 1:27). It is allowing Christ to "life out"
the Christian life *through* me. It is admitting that I can-

1

not make my marriage work, but that Christ through me is able to make it work.

Therein lies the missing ingredient; yet thousands of believers are at a loss and through personal failure have discovered that they *cannot live* a consistent, *agape* lifestyle toward their spouse. Most are trying to "do their best with God's help," either because they have never been exposed to the reality of the Biblical method, or they do not understand how to practically "life it out." In their failure, they have been prepared by the Holy Spirit for the answer in this book; that is, "Christ in you, the hope of glory" (Colossians 1:27).

There are but two ways a Christian can operate: He can walk "in the Spirit" or "after the flesh." Heretofore, I'd always thought there were *three* ways. "In the Spirit" meant teaching Sunday School and helping little old ladies across the street, and "after the flesh" meant lusting after women. These polarities comprised part of my time, but most of my life was lived in a large third area which I called "my way." It involved my work-a-day world—eating, playing with my kids, watching ball games, etc.—all of which I considered neither sinful nor spiritual.

The problem with my approach to life was that the Bible said nothing about this third way. It spoke only of two ways, in the Spirit and after the flesh. My third way, as I have described it, was after the flesh as well. In fact, I discovered to my horror that even what I *thought* was walking in the Spirit (teaching Sunday School) was walking after the flesh, because my method was wrong. My entire life was being lived on "flesh power."

Why did Jesus come *into* you instead of alongside, under, behind, or before you? Listen carefully; Jesus is the only one who could ever live the Christian life. He came *into* you in order to express the life of Christ *through* you. There it is, sweet and simple. That's the new plan as old as the New Testament.

If both Anabel and I could understand how to do this, what kind of marriage would we be *guaranteed?* Why, we could take this show on the road and write a book about it! The trick is understanding *how* to let Christ live His life through you.

> . . . do not go on presenting the members of your body to sin as instruments of unrighteousness; but present yourselves to God as those alive from the dead, and your members as instruments of righteousness to God. (Romans 6:13)

There are those two ways again. I either present myself to God or to sin. Chapters 5-8 of Romans contain the word "sin" forty-one times. Here's an amazing fact: Forty of those times it is a noun; only once is it a verb! Did you grasp that? It's a *noun* in the verse above. But if, as you just read it, you interpreted "sin" as a verb (i.e., stealing hubcaps or the like), then you just missed one of the most powerful truths in the New Testament. There are dozens of verses in the New Testament where sin is a noun, not a verb (to be sinning), and if you interpret sin in those verses as verbs, you've taken the wrong exit off the freeway.

In his classic and highly recognized work, *Expository Dictionary of New Testament Words*, W. E. Vine states that in eleven of these forty instances sin is a "governing power or principle" which is "personified" (p. 1055). What does that mean? It means the word *sin* is a power which is "represented as a person." Let's see if we can clarify that.

In the verse I quoted, let's represent this power called sin as a person. We'll let sin be personified as a sergeant, and you are a private under his authority. Now when a sergeant says "frog," a private jumps. He has no choice because a private is under the authority of a sergeant. The only thing that could break "Sgt. Sin's" hold on you would be either the termination of his authority or the termination of your obligation to that authority, or perhaps both. Let's take, for instance, death. Should Sgt. Sin die, that would free you from his authority; and if you died, you would certainly be out from under his dictatorial ways. Either way, someone would have to die in order for you to be set free.

> Knowing this, that our old self was crucified with Him . . . (Romans 6:6). (You died.)

> . . . he who has died is freed from sin [the noun] (Romans 6:7). (Your death freed you from sin's ability to make you obey. You have now, in a sense,

been reborn as a civilian free from the sergeant's authority.)

. . . consider yourselves to be dead to sin [the noun], but alive to God in Christ Jesus (Romans 6:11). (You are under a new system; thus, you must act dead to the sergeant and alive to your freedom.)

You died in Christ when He was crucified (Romans 6:6). Then you were reborn as a new person in Christ at His resurrection (see 2 Corinthians 5:17). This comes with the package when you get saved. Water baptism is a pantomime portrayal of it (Romans 6:4). As this new spirit-being, you are no longer under Sgt. Sin's authority. You have a new Master, Jesus! Your death effected a permanent liberation from sin's (the noun) tyrannical authority over you. You don't have to pay any attention to Sgt. Sin now.

Picture the "Sarge" screaming in your ear, demanding that you hit the deck and pick up cigarette butts with your teeth while doing fifty push-ups. Picture the new you, born anew (not the old private raised from the dead) grinning and saying, "Rain on you, Sarge. *You have no authority over me.* I am dead to you." Dear people, that is precisely our new relationship to this power the Bible calls "sin."

Now, let's give old Sgt. Sin a couple of aces in the hole. He doesn't give up that easily. He knows that your *brain* was programmed from the years spent under his authority, and although you may be a new civilian, your brain is programmed with old Marine ways. (The Bible calls these old ways "flesh" [see Philippians 3:3-9].) If Sarge could somehow infiltrate your brain, and if he could be *personified* as the *old* private who used to submit so readily to his authority, then he could constantly "talk" to the new you as though you were still in the Marine Corps and under his control! He'd employ your old Marine ways, *use first singular pronouns, and speak to you with your own accent.* This way you would be deceived into thinking you were reasoning things out in your *own* mind. In every situation, moment by moment, that you encounter, Sgt. Sin "speaks" to you, masquerading as the old private, intimidating, tempting, accusing, badgering, deceiving you into *behaving just like you were still a Marine.* He'd finally get you so confused that you'd be convinced you have two personalities, a civilian one (good) and a Marine one (evil). If Sgt. Sin were skilled enough, he might even be able to convince you that you had never become a civilian at all!

I made an astounding discovery one time. For every verse in the New Testament which speaks of Christ indwelling the believer, there are *ten* verses which state that the believer is *in* Jesus!

The verses which pertain to my indwelling Jesus refer to my death and new birth *in Him.* Your essence is spirit. *You are a spiritual creature in an earthsuit, not a physical creature with a spirit.* God changed you by killing the old spirit-man and starting all over again, not physically, but spiritually.

Look up all the "in Christ" terms in Scripture (i.e., "in Christ," "in Him," "in Jesus," "in Whom," etc.) and take note of the verb tenses and descriptive phrases God uses to speak of you now that you are a "new creature" *in* Christ (see 2 Corinthians 5:17). Since this is how God *now* describes you, it supersedes any of the world's personality tests, the opinions of others, and even those you hold toward yourself. Your new birth in Jesus is your *true* identity now and throughout all eternity. Embracing this as reality is the critical key to your victory over "Sgt. Sin."

Look at some of the Biblical evidence that Christians have died and been reborn as new people, not retread jobs. Jesus said you can't sew a new patch on an old garment (see Luke 5:36). He was saying there is no way you can be a Marine and a civilian simultaneously. Jesus said you can't pour new wine into an old skin or it'll rupture (see Mark 2:22). He was saying you can't pour the Holy Spirit into the old Marine. He'll leak! Only civilians can hold Him (see Ezekiel 36:26-27). The Word says you can't mix light with darkness (see 2 Corinthians 6:14), yet we've been deceived into believing that Christians are a mixture of light and darkness within.

Jesus stated, with reference to Satan's kingdom, "any kingdom [city or house] divided against itself shall not stand" (Matthew 12:25b); yet, we Christians have naively believed that each of us was recreated as a "house divided against itself," half civilian and half Marine. I ask you, would God, who "called you *out* of darkness *into* His marvelous light" (1 Peter 2:9, emphasis added), deliberately set you up for a "cannot stand" situation by creating you as a house divided against itself?†

Dear Christian, you are not fighting a civil war. That Marine inside you is not *you*. It is the noun sin masquerading as the *old* you; it's Sgt. Sin *impersonating the old man* who was crucified with Christ. He's the "fly in the ointment" and that's the reason it *seems* like the old man is still alive.

There is something tragically different between the twentieth-century practice of Christianity and that of the first century Christians. Our intimate loved ones and even our high-profile heroes of the faith are falling like flies! God help us! If the heroes can't make it, who can? By the grace of God, the ones who can make it are the ones who discover and appropriate the "mystery . . . which is Christ in you" (Colossians 1:27); they are those who discover they cannot live the Christian life, but that the One who lives within them can. The trick is discovering our *true* identity *in* Christ, *why* He indwells us, and *how* to let Him live through us to overcome Sgt. Sin.

---

† A thorough treatment of the truth of our identity in Christ and its practical application is available in Bill Gillham, *Lifetime Guarantee*, (Brentwood, TN: Wolgemuth & Hyatt, Publishers, 1988). It is imperative that Christians appropriate the reality of this truth if we are to walk in victory through these dark days.

Now, let's see just how this truth is going to enable us to make our marriages work.

1

FLESH WED TO FLESH EQUALS DISASTER

*B*ILL: Anabel and I would like to invite you to sit down with us at our kitchen table while we discuss how our marriage and yours can bring honor to Jesus. Come on in and pull up a chair.

We bought this round oak table at a used furniture store for five dollars when we first married. It had a large burned spot on the top, so we laminated it with this pale blue, linen-textured formica, and then refinished the base. You can see by our kitchen that Anabel likes powder blue.

We got that butcher block out of a school, years ago. What a mess it was! And the shelf on the brick wall is an example of my shelf-making you've heard me tell about in our Victorious Christian Living Seminar tapes. I especially like that milk bottle sitting on the shelf that has the slogan "Buy More War Bonds"; I found it in a trash pile. Anabel did the punched tin work on the cabinet doors behind you. As you can see, we like an old-fashioned decor.

Sitting here in the middle of all these things we've collected and worked on reminds us of the things we need to share about our roles in marriage. You might want to make some notes as we talk. We may not cover each specific question you have about marriage, but we'll try to be pretty comprehensive.

First of all, we must understand that God has certain laws He has established on earth, such as the law of gravity. It's for our good; it enables airplanes to fly, keeps us from falling off the planet, keeps our houses on the ground, etc. But if you violate it, you'll go splat.

God also has certain laws which He has designed for us as husband and wife. He is not an arbitrary Person. Marriage roles, like gravity, are designed for our good and if we violate them, something is going to go splat. It may be us, the marriage, or the kids, but something is going to suffer until we get our "ducks lined up" according to what He says. Hey, the job description of a god is, "He runs things." There is only one true God and if we are ever to experience His peace, we must let Him rule us. He will never let me "enter into His rest" as long as I'm making up my own rules.

Honey, why don't you tell them where we're getting this information on our roles in marriage. Did we just figure it out for ourselves?

ANABEL: No, we got these truths from God's Word. When we began to search the Bible to see just what *you* needed as a husband, we didn't look in our concordance under "husband," but under "wife." God wouldn't tell me, as your wife, to do something for you that you don't have a need for, so if we look under the word "wife," we'll discover what the wife is to do in order to meet the husband's needs.

Similarly, when you are searching the Bible to discover what I need as your wife, you look up the verses containing the word "husband." These will spell out what you are to do for me and reveal my needs as your bride.

BILL: We certainly were not meeting each other's needs in the early years of our marriage; indeed, I couldn't even verbalize what mine were. I just knew I was a frustrated, unhappy man.

ANABEL: We were both hurting. Let me review a typical scene from the first few years of our blissful married life.

Mother and Dad are coming for a visit. Company. And of course, when company comes I want the house to be just perfect. I need to have the rods put up for some new curtains, but asking Bill to do things like that just never seems to turn out all that well. (That's putting it mildly!)

I finally take "one giant step" and broach the subject, and it's just like I thought it would be—he's "wormy" about it. Oh, he condescends to do it, but every word and every move indicate that this is certainly *not* something that he enjoys. I can just imagine what's going on in his mind: *No woman tells me what to do. Why does she have to put up silly curtains anyway? Dumb woman. She's always trying to control my time.*

And I'm getting more anxious. *Oh, Lord, don't let him hit his finger or bend the nail. Please don't let anything go wrong.* I am very conscious of my every move. I want to be sure to hand him the hammer with the handle rotated in the right direction. Oh, I've forgotten which direction is the right direction!

"Could you please hand that hammer to me the right way?"

"I'm sorry."

"Well, I've told you how to do it ten times. I don't see why you have to have me work on these silly curtains. The windows looked okay like they were."

By now there's a lump in my throat, and my emotions are threatening to spill out all over the place—not exactly what I had in mind for my folks' visit!

BILL: Now, why in the world would I be acting like such a hammerhead? And why would Anabel be so insecure and scared in our relationship? To answer those questions, we'd like you to meet Mr. Threatened Macho Flesh and Mrs. Super Sensitivity Flesh—Bill and Anabel. We want to explain our "flesh patterns" to you and show how walking in them nearly destroyed our marriage.

I'm going to begin with my childhood so you can see how my flesh was developed. Mom and Pop made some mistakes, but I cannot blame my folks for my hang-ups. I generated those hang-ups striving to get my needs met in their home. I love them and wouldn't change my past because I am now able to see it as being a part of my pilgrimage with Christ.

Let me explain just how children are patterned before I continue. God is Love, so He created you with a basic human need to be loved. That's good, because if you didn't need love, you wouldn't need God. When you showed up on Planet Earth you knew nothing of God, so *you* set out to satisfy your need for love. You drew an imaginary circle around yourself, declared *yourself* god (ruler) of *your* circle and made up your own rules, striving to get your needs met. I call it playing "lord of the ring." That's the definition of original sin.

A little baby is a totally self-centered "lord of the ring". If he awakens at 2:00 A.M. cold, wet, and hungry, does he lie there and think, *Poor Mom. I just can't make her get up again tonight. She needs her rest. I'll just tough it out until daylight?* No way! *Hey! Wake up! Come fix the kid!*

Because of this self-centeredness, he learns only about *himself* from the feedback he gets from others; he does not learn about *them*. If his folks do not kiss him, he does not learn that it's difficult for them to show affection; he learns, *I'm unkissable. Who'd want to kiss me?* He's choreographing his ring.

Your emotions respond to your mind. Set your mind on a fearful stimulus, like a snarling Doberman pinscher, and you'll *feel* fearful. Set your mind that you're unkissable, and you'll feel unkissable. Set your mind there consistently, and on a one-to-ten scale, your "feeler" will become stuck on an eight. By the time you are five years old, all the points beneath the eight will erode away. Because you *feel* unkissable at level eight most of the time, you'll set your mind on how you feel and believe it's true. Your "flesh patterns" are being programmed into your brain.

Now back to me and how my patterns developed. As a little boy, I needed to learn to accept myself as male. What do I mean? I mean that at age six I needed to feel I could kick a ball better than a girl, that I could sweat more than she could, that I could handle snakes, etc. That's male. In short, I needed to feel that I was the stronger of the genders. God made me this way. It's not an ego trip; it's being a male. It's as normal for boys to be that way as it is for girls to want to wear their mothers' high-heeled shoes.

Mom and Pop's biggest mistake in their marriage was establishing it contrary to God's plan in that Mom "lifed out" the role of husband, and Pop the role of wife. She dominated Pop and he submitted to her authority over him. He was a very passive man, and that's upside down to God's plan. If I ever asked him permission to do anything, he'd say, "Go ask your mom." I finally rejected him as my male role model and quit asking him. I didn't want him in my ring. He didn't fit my plan.

Mom represented *female* to me as she was the main female to whom I related, so learning to accept myself as male meant I had to see myself as progressing toward becoming stronger than Mom. That looked like climbing Mt. Everest! Nobody was stronger than *my* mother. We called her "strong as an acre of garlic"—behind her back.

Some sons are so intimidated in a setting like this that, with a lot of help from the devil, they do a 180° turn and become homosexual. Others semi-surrender their masculinity and go passive like my dad did when he was a kid. They go through life submitting to everyone, never making waves and thus hoping to gain acceptance. Others rebel at their mom's dominance over them and fight back; they disdain their dad's passivity and reject him as a role model. They set out to prove their masculinity to *themselves*, and they become macho.

As I played lord of my ring, I was striving to be masculine. How could I prove my masculinity to *myself*? I could become vulgar and profane. I could become an athlete, earn a letter jacket, work at developing a "don't-tread-on-me" look in my eyes, strive to be a mean-machine. This was pretty difficult because of my earthsuit; at age fifteen it was 52"and weighed 110 lbs. Oh, but I tried.

What else could I do? I could seduce the high school girls. That's macho. The problem was that no one ever kissed anybody in our family. Mom didn't even let the dog lick us, man. So I learned about *myself*. I *felt* unkissy. My feeler was stuck. So not only did I not get into sex, I had to struggle to get into kiss! All my sexual encounters took place in my thought-life, and that kind of thinking would eventually plague me in my adult life as a Christian. I was choreographing my flesh patterns.

One group of people evolved into my arch enemies. They were a constant reminder to me of my weakness and inability to accept myself as a *real* male. Who were they? Strong, outspoken, assertive women. They threatened my masculinity just like Mom. I spewed my internal frustration onto them in the form of insults, sarcasm, criticism, and ridicule. They were blocking me from accepting myself. They messed up my ring.

Then I got married. What sort of a woman did I marry? One who would relieve the pressure, right? Wrong. I married one who was strong as an acre of garlic. You ask, "Well, Delbert Dumb, why did you do that?" *Because my feeler was stuck!* I *felt* like a boy trying to enter a man's world with a man's responsibilities, and I couldn't hack it, so I married someone who could carry the load of both roles in the relationship. Then when she did so well, it ate my lunch! So after the honeymoon was over, I began to unleash this never-ending supply of hostility against females onto my precious wife. I tried to destroy her.

After I got saved at age twenty-nine, all this garbage became my "old ways," my unique version of the *flesh*. I had programmed my brain with it. With salvation, my behavior changed in many ways, but the old hostility and criticism of Anabel actually seemed to get worse. I was walking after the flesh, and I had no idea how to escape from it. I was a personal soul winner in the public eye, but a destroyer in my own home. And I couldn't quit. . . .

Finally, after thirteen years of frustration from trying to live the Christian life, God brought me to the end of *my* resources. He showed me through my weakness that He didn't put Christ in me to help me, but to express *His* Life *through* me. Experiencing the failure of my own ability to carry me through the deepest crises in my life proved to be the key to discovering Christ *as* my Life.

Honey, tell them about your flesh and how it developed.

ANABEL: During those traumatic years of our marriage, an outside observer would have looked at me and said, "She doesn't have any problems." But to me, life was a bottomless pit with oil-slick walls and quicksand on the bottom where my feverish flailing only caused me to sink in further. I couldn't bail myself out of the awful hole I was in. I was unhappy. Frustrated. Hurting. Barely surviving.

I went into marriage with some very positive attributes. I was an efficient, outgoing, self-confident person with an impressive record: junior high Student Council representative, senior high Student Council president, drum major, valedictorian, voted most popular girl on campus in college — I was "performing" well.

You see, my pattern was for performance-based acceptance, and after years of walking in PBA, one generally evolves toward a performance-based self-acceptance. Now, if someone is a performer, then nine chances out of ten she is also a perfectionist. And when she is a perfectionist, she is usually very sensitive to any kind of evaluative criticism. "Don't tell me that I did it wrong. I did not. I did it perfectly. In fact, I did it six times just to be sure it was done perfectly."

It is important to realize that as a super performer I demanded perfect performance out of myself. (Bill did not demand perfect performance out of himself; rather, he demanded it out of the people around him, people who were to meet his needs. This is one of the characteristics of a person with "indulged flesh" patterns.) These two patterns, being a super performer/perfectionist and being supersensitive about critical remarks, nearly destroyed me, my marriage, and my family.

My techniques for getting acceptance and love in the years before marriage had been very successful. A performer is driven to achieve, and though I was discouraged when I didn't do well, there was always another tomorrow, another chance, another place. But this was it! The big event—marriage—and I wasn't winning! I was being torn down and, to top it all, I couldn't get out of this "contest" and enter another one.

During my years in school, I had learned to protect my image by never having any close friends; I didn't want anyone ever to see me when I was not "up" and performing well. You see, my mind-set was that people would not accept or like me if I did not perform well enough to please them; and now, in my marriage, this mind-set had been validated. Bill *knew* me. My fears were justified. You get to know me, and you won't like me. Bill didn't like me. My techniques weren't working anymore, and my self-esteem began to plummet.

I didn't pray about the person I was to marry. Bill and I dated steadily for five years. We were constant companions. Surely you know someone after being constant companions for five years. I knew Bill. That is, I *thought* I knew Bill. He was very thoughtful, considerate, and kind. He never cursed or told off-color stories. He was simply "Mr. Wonderful." Then we got married, and when he got me into the castle with the drawbridge up, this tender, pure, considerate, thoughtful, kind young man changed incredibly.

The most horrible change was in the way he talked to me, the things he said to me. I never shall forget one Saturday morning in our first little honeymoon apartment. Bill said, "Honey, I'd like to talk to you for a moment." He took me by the hand and led me into our living room. We sat down on the little flowered settee, and he said to me, very gently, "Honey, I wish that you would learn to do at least *one thing* well."

I thought I was doing pretty well, but obviously I wasn't. Now if Bill expected this to destroy me (remember his game plan was to destroy strong, capable women), then his expectations were wrong. His criticism motivated me to do bigger and better and more perfect things. You see, I was trying to get Bill to praise me. The lifeblood of a performer is praise. If you don't get it, you begin to die. So I was engaged in a life-and-death battle—and I was losing. Oh, but I was going to fight!

For instance, when Bill moonlighted in the oil fields during his summer break from teaching, he would leave the house at 7:30 in the morning and get home at 4:30 or 5:00, dirty, tired, hungry, and in a bad mood. My thinking was: What can I do for Bill today to please him? I know, I'll mow and edge the lawn, prune the hedges, and rake everything up. Then, when he comes home, he'll say, "Would you look at this lawn. Talk about manicured! Did you do all of this by yourself, Honey? How great it looks!" Surely he will notice and praise me, I think. But, no, he didn't.

Good performer that I am, I didn't give up. I was starving for praise. I would try harder tomorrow; I knew what I'd do. I'd have a freezer of his favorite ice cream sitting on the porch, and when he saw it he would say, "What a wife you are! I can't think of anything that would please me more than a dish of ice cream right now." He *would* say something like that, wouldn't he? But he didn't.

Another tomorrow. Another "try" day. My new plan is to start saving pennies from our very meager budget and buy some steaks. Then, when Bill sits down to the supper table, he will say, "What a marvel you are with this budget, Honey. To think that you could save enough money to have a supper like this. I am so proud of you." He will . . . won't he . . . please? No, he won't.

BILL: Honey, as we are able now to look back on this horror story and analyze it, we can see what was happening to us. I was very insecure in my masculinity and was trying to stamp out every evidence or "proof" that my fears were valid. You were striving to perform, twice as well as anyone should be expected to perform, in order to get praise from me and to preserve your self-esteem. So we were the immovable object meeting the indestructible force, and through it all, we crashed in flames.

ANABEL: I am so thankful that we have been given some insight into our behavior. But there's more. Bill couldn't destroy me by criticizing my performance. I was too strong for him, so he eventually switched plans. He began pointing out things that I couldn't change. For instance, one time we were going to a square dance and I, of course, looked "perfect." (Performers always look perfect. They don't get out of the house until they do!) Bill looked over at me in my frilly square-dance dress and said, "You know, I really can't imagine anyone wanting to dance with you." I didn't enjoy the square dance.

Or we would be walking out the door for an evening of fun, and he would casually say, "Honey, try not to laugh so much this evening. You really make people uncomfortable when you do that." His tactics began to work, and his game plan for destroying Anabel was showing signs of success.

After seven years of marriage, Bill became a Christian. He began to realize, after all those years, the person he had become and he called out to God. God heard him and knew the depths of his desire, the sincerity of his heart, and responded to his cry of repentance. That man is no more, but it was not an "overnight" miracle — his horrible sarcastic tongue remained.

Let's look twenty years into the marriage. I had not given up, but by then I had developed a coping mechanism for existing. Depression. Deep depression. You can't remember anything nice happening yesterday, and you have no hope that something nice will happen tomorrow. You just have today, and I had learned from the man I live with that I do not perform well on todays, so I wanted out. The only acceptable "out" for a performer is suicide. That way you don't have to face people after your poor performance.

This was my life when the Lord spoke to me. Oh, I wanted our marriage to work so badly. I had read and reread Ephesians 5:33b from the Amplified Bible about respecting and loving and honoring your husband. I couldn't do all of those things. I didn't even *like* Bill.

I had gone to bed. It had been a bad day. I don't remember why, because I had a lot of bad days. I was sobbing and talking to the Lord: "God, I don't understand what is going on in my life. My marriage is so far from what I long for it to be and what I know You intended it to be. My kids are not turning out the way I want them to, and Lord, I am so tired. I'm weary. I've given and given and given, and I just don't think that I can give anymore. (Then I said something that I had never said in all of my forty some-odd years, something that is very difficult for a performer to say.) *Lord, I give up. I can't do it.* If anything is going to come of this marriage, if anything is going to come out of these kids, You're going to have to do it; I can't."

God spoke to me that night. (I mean that thoughts came to mind that were foreign to my way of thinking, and because of what they said to me, I by faith believe it was the Lord.) It was a simple little phrase: "Thank you, Anabel. I'll do it all for you." That was the beginning, and I do mean beginning. Step by step by sometimes painful step, I have learned and am learning the truth of Galatians 2:20:

I have been crucified with Christ; and it is no longer I who live, but Christ lives in me; and the life which I now live in the flesh [as the wife of Bill Gillham, as the mother of Pres, Mace, Will, and Wade, whether I am teaching, making a banana cream pie, digging in the marigolds or cleaning the commode] I live by faith in the Son of God, who loved me, and delivered Himself up for me.

And what an incredible difference that has made in my life!

Bill: Those *were* hard times, weren't they? They were hard for both of us, and as you tell your story, Sugar, I plead guilty to wearing the "black hat." I ought to have been shot. I was destroying you with my critical tongue, and you were destroying me with your strength. We were mutually destroying each other, weren't we? We did not understand how to let Christ live through us in order to straighten out the mess we had created.

2

SERIOUSLY, IS MARRIAGE FOR REAL?

B ILL: I read an article some time ago which quoted a statistic that shocked me: The clergy ranked third among professional groups in rate of divorce!† I believe this is because many of these dear people do not know how to let Jesus express His life through them in order to make their marriages work. They are trying to do it in

† Mary LaGrand Bouma, "Ministers' Wives: The Walking Wounded," *Leadership*, Winter 1980, 51.

their *own* strength with God's *help*, and that invalidates God's warranty.

ANABEL: Yes, Honey, but God's Biblical model for marriage is considered essentially archaic today. We have such warped views of marriage in our culture. First, there is the *fantasy* approach. Our kids are bombarded constantly via the movies and television with fantasy relationships. Love is one great romantic fling—passion that never seems to wane—and if it does, you move on to another relationship. It is so difficult to convince two kids with stars in their eyes that Prince Charming and Sleeping Beauty exist only in fairy tales and that the absolute bottom line of marriage is spelled C-O-M-M-I-T-M-E-N-T. You have to work at it. Love does not hold your marriage together. It is marriage that holds the love together.

Then there is the *casual* approach. Even as the groom is standing at the altar watching this vision of loveliness float down the aisle, one or both of them may have in the back of their minds this thought: "If it doesn't work out, we can always get a divorce." It's that socially acceptable today. There's no stigma attached anymore. It's so easy to say, "I'm unhappy with you. I didn't know it was going to be this way. I don't want to live with you anymore." And another divorce statistic rings up.

I suppose, Honey, that the warped view we see the most of is "building separate lives." If the wife could verbalize her thoughts, she might say: "I really don't mind, Husband, that you jet all over the country, that you are in London one week and Lisbon the next." Or, "It doesn't really bother me that your territory now covers four states and that you're gone the majority of the time." Or, "I don't care if you play softball three nights a week and go fishing every weekend. That's okay with me. You see, Husband, I get along better without you than I do with you. I don't need you. I've given up on you. I've built my own life. I have bridge club on Tuesdays, Bible Study Fellowship Leader's Meeting on Monday, Bible Study Fellowship every Wednesday, hospital volunteer duty every Thursday, jogging on Monday, Wednesday and Friday, museum and fine arts committee meeting monthly—So you see, I don't really need you anymore." Or perhaps, "My career is very satisfying to me. I find great fulfillment in it, and I believe I'm making a difference in my world. My life is now very fulfilled without you."

BILL: When we describe these views in our seminars, couples laugh with us and say, "Oh, we wave to each other as we meet in the driveway, but that's about it." Someone said it this way: "We are held together by thin strands of thread called 'the children,' or 'our financial status,' or 'our reputation in the community.'" They know nothing of the beautiful oneness God intended for us to experience in our marriages. How sad. . . .

ANABEL: The following letter reveals how the heartbreak grows.

Dear Anabel,

With John and me there was nothing. We compromised and worked our way through a million crises, but after at least ten years of just sharing the same house, where even idle conversation ended in raw nerves, what can we do but call it quits?

I sat down and wrote "What Went Wrong Along the Way," at the top of a piece of typing paper the day before the divorce was final. I wrote for three and one-half hours before I quit. It was a gradual twenty-year process. Oh, we were very happy when my whole world revolved around him and his work.

I think this has had a lot to do with our growing apart. It was a very subtle, deep-down, hairline crack in the dike that simply grew and grew. He pulled within himself and built a wall that was rarely opened to me. I shrugged it off and went out into my world of music and church-caring people and in the quiet times felt lonely. That, of course, was only part of the problem, but it was a major part. Togetherness is so important, as you well know, and John and I *never* did anything together. Most people didn't even know I had a husband because I was always alone. And he was always alone when he went somewhere — which was seldom. So we were both lonely people who just lived together.

It doesn't surprise us that young people live together outside the marriage vows. "If living with someone for six or eight months will keep me from getting into the hell that my parents glibly called marriage, then I'll try it with no strings attached."

Then there is the view of marriage that was espoused from pulpits not too many years ago and is still held to tenaciously by some. It glorifies this very gifted, grand and noble male who puts up with, indeed, endures this little timid, mealy-mouthed, mousy nonentity called the female.

Honey, I looked up the word "nonentity" just to be sure it communicated what I wanted. Do you know what the word means?

BILL: What?

ANABEL: It means a person or thing of little or no importance.

BILL: Yeah, she's like an empty catsup bottle or something. I remember one time years ago when the pastor cited a particular couple in our fellowship as the epitome of what a Christian marriage ought to be; we were exhorted to emulate their example. I'll call this couple John and Mary. I had been in their home that very week to see how their redecorating was progressing.

"What color are you going to paint your kitchen, Mary?" I asked.

"I don't know. John hasn't told me yet," she responded.

That was fairly typical of their interaction. You got the idea that when John was hungry he'd snap his fingers and say, "kitchen," and she'd fire out to build him a sandwich. At times, I guess he'd snap his fingers and say, "bedroom." She operated at about the same level as a good cocker spaniel.

Folks, as I understand the Bible, that example of passivity is not what God has in mind for a wife. I believe that dear, young wife would have interacted with her husband in that same manner if she had never met Jesus. That's not Christian submission; it's "chicken flesh." She operated out of a fear of men. (Incidentally, I'm happy to report that John and Mary have turned things around now through understanding how to appropriate Christ as life.)

ANABEL: How did she become so passive? Some people may think she was just born that way.

BILL: No, she developed it herself. As a child she learned that by submitting to all power figures, both male and female, she could gain their acceptance and love. The more she submitted, the less friction she experienced; and for her, the lesser the friction meant the greater the love and acceptance.

Her goal was to "never make waves." If she ever stated an opinion and sensed it was rejected by another, she took it personally, believing they were rejecting *her*. Finding that very unpleasant, she developed the practice of never expressing an opinion. Finally she arrived at the point where she didn't even know what her opinion was a great deal of the time. As we'd say back home, "She became anybody's dog that would hunt with her."

Question: Is that who she is *now* as a new woman in Christ, or is that now her unique version of the flesh? It's her "old ways" which the Bible calls "flesh." God did not give birth to a *passive* new man or woman in Christ. That passivity is a do-it-yourself project. True Biblical submission differs from passivity.

I recall a woman in her forties who came up to me after I had spoken at a couples retreat in Florida. She was tentative in her manner, glancing around as she tearfully related how she had always been a "submissive wife," but that her husband, a godly man whom she dearly loved, had a terrible temper. She assured me that she had never mentioned this to "any living soul," then went on to say that when he lost his temper and yelled at her, it just crushed her. Her custom, after Sam's angry explosions, was to go quietly to her bedroom and cry, never letting him see her reaction.

She said she had committed what seemed an unpardonable sin three months ago when, following one of his tirades, she confronted him by saying, "Sam, I just can't handle your temper any longer! I don't think I can keep going like this. I feel like it's eventually going to kill me. I'm having severe headaches."

"Then I just fell apart crying; and I've always been such a submissive wife. I just don't know how I could have done such a terrible thing." She wept quietly into her handkerchief.

"What did Sam say when you confronted him like that?"

"He took me in his arms and held me and said he was so sorry he had been hurting me all these years and that he wouldn't hurt me for the world. He hasn't lost his temper since! But, I just *feel* so bad for having done that; I've *always* been a submissive wife and I know I've failed the Lord. I just don't know what made me do such a thing."

"How did Sam feel about his temper problem?"

"Oh, he has grieved over it."

I said, "Sweet Sister, *Agape* means 'I will *do* the most redemptive, edifying, constructive thing I can think of for you.' Some Christians will disagree with me, but I want to give you a minority report. I believe you were under the control of the Holy Spirit when you said what you did to Sam. God had to bring you to the point of such utter despair, frustration, and even anger so that you would be motivated to confront your husband. He's been wanting to do this through you for years, and He has demonstrated that it was *God at work through you* by the change in Sam's behavior. It won't always work out this way, but God did this to give you *proof* that He was working through you.

"Now you are letting Sgt. Sin accuse you when all you did was to *agape* your husband, and you are believing it's the Holy Spirit convicting you. No!

That's false guilt. You didn't rebel; you *loved* Sam. It was a courageous thing you did for him.

"All these years you have been operating from your stuck feeler on a 'fear-of-man' basis. All your life your lord-of-the-ring technique has been never to make waves because of a fear of rejection. Much of your passive submission was not godly, rather it was on the basis of a fear that you'd lose your husband's love by making him upset with you. That's your flesh."

ANABEL: I agree with what you told her, Honey, but sometimes men *are* responsible for our feelings of fear and our passive behavior just as they sometimes make us feel like nonentities by implying that the work we do around the house is unimportant. They come through like the husband in the cartoon I saw one time who said, "You stick to your washing, ironing, cooking and scrubbing. No wife of mine is going to work!" Housekeeping is labeled a "trivial pursuit." The propaganda that inundates me in the world system goes something like this:

"You really should place your child in a day-care center. It will so enhance his social adjustment, and he will then quickly acclimate to elementary school."

Wow! There goes my role as mother that I thought was so very important, so much so that I would actually keep my little one out of school an extra year so that I might instill in him *my* standards, *my* moral values, *my* deep convictions. That's been taken away from me. It isn't really all that important anymore.

Then I hear the subtle suggestions that it would really enhance our sex life if my husband could have sort of a "sexual smorgasbord" with several partners. Just any woman can give sexual satisfaction—sometimes much more effectively than a wife with Victorian standards.

And there goes that very intimate relationship that I thought was just mine . . . that no other woman would ever know. It was to be a very special relationship that only I would have, and as my husband and I would look at each other across a crowded room, there would be a secret message in our eyes—he would know me as no other man would. That's gone. It isn't important anymore.

And, of course, advertisers give me the message that having the right bottle under the sink means just any clod can keep house, step out the door in record-breaking time, and looking back at a shiny floor, find *true* fulfillment as they enter the *real* working world. I am *not* a *house*keeper; I am a home*maker*! There's an incredible difference. The job classification does not revolve around "trivia." You know, when there are a lot of ladies together and they have to introduce themselves and tell what they do, those who don't work outside the home feel pressured to come up with something that sounds better than, "I just stay at home." So we call ourselves something clever like "domestic engineers" or "household maintenance experts." Oh, no—we are wives and mothers, and our home is a major tool in our kit for being effective in our role.

It's important for my sons to smell cookies baking when they come in from school. It's important for my husband to smell supper cooking (even if it's just an onion in the oven). We don't seem to realize that a child's concept of home is what he *experiences* as home. I am training my boys in "what-I-want-in-a-wife"; I am teaching my daughter how to function in the role of wife and mother. I'm building a refuge, a haven. I'm creating a place where my husband does not have to compete, where order prevails, and where pressures are alleviated somewhat. I'm giving my children a place of security wrapped in and governed by love.

But all of that has been taken away from women. So they have come out with their fists clenched, saying, "I *am* somebody, and I will prove it to you, man. I will do whatever you do as well as you do or better than you do. I am *not* a nonentity!"

BILL: And you know, Honey, I bear my share of the responsibility for driving the women to that position of frustration through my "macho flesh" behavior. I plead guilty, and I'm truly sorry. But two wrongs don't make a right, do they?

ANABEL: No. You said it at the beginning of this chapter: Too many of us try to make our marriage work by our own strength when we just need to understand our God-ordained roles. A woman is never in a position of inferiority when she is in the role God created for her.

BILL: Does that mean that a wife and mom can never be in God's will if she's gainfully employed?

ANABEL: No. That is a question which I'm often asked by women. Many will cite the "Proverbs Thirty-One Woman" as a Scriptural role model of a wife who was a very successful businesswoman. However, as you read about her lifestyle and begin to see her as your wife/career woman role model, be sure to place a retinue of servants in her home and understand that her husband "sits in the gate." This means he's a community leader and is very successful. He is not passive, nor is he a threatened male. That makes an incredible difference.

Some women *have* to work. They are the sole bread-winner in a fragmented family. Others have to work because of certain existing circumstances in their lives. They have no choice. I understand that.

But, the Bible clarifies the role of the woman *who has a choice*. If you can fulfill your Biblical role of wife and your Biblical role of mother (both of which you *volitionally* chose), not neglecting those things which He has assigned you, and still have time left to pursue a career outside the home, then it would be acceptable to pursue that goal as well.

As a wife and mother under God's authority, I have established my priorities from His Word. The pressures of our culture are increasing the stress upon all of us in these last days. The demands placed upon me seem almost to scream out that they have a right to be number one in my life. I must use the Bible as *the* criterion if I am to walk with God and maintain His inner peace. Let me list these priorities for you in their Biblical order:†

Priorities

1. A growing, vital, personal relationship with Christ

2. A wife

3. A mother

4. My earthly family

5. Using the gifts God gave me for service, be it in my home or at my job

6. Special people He has brought into my life

7. My church family

8. The hurting world

I have been a part-time employee of Gillham Ministries Inc. (GMI) for many years. I find it is acceptable to Bill and to me only when we keep the perspective that I am a part-time GMI employee, and I am a full-time wife and mother. Bill's help and understanding in this respect are invaluable.

---

† See Appendix A for an elaboration on these.

BILL: When in doubt, refer to the Manufacturer's Instructions, right? So, let's go to the Bible and see what God has to say about how He intends for a marriage to be put together. Genesis 2:18 says, "Then the Lord God said, 'It is not good for the man to be alone; I will make him a helper suitable for him.'" The Amplified translation says, "completing him." The literal rendition is "corresponding to him."

Let's draw a picture of Adam (see Figure 2.1). God took a look at him and said, "Now that's not going to fly. That guy is like an eight-cylinder car that's only hitting on four. I've got to make a second person to complete him." So He made Eve, placed them together, said they were now "one," said all of it was "very good," and closed up the creating shop (see Figure 2.2).

This brings up an interesting question. I wonder if one of these two people is basically superior to the other? Well, let's not divide up into small groups to discuss it. Let's go to the Bible to see if we can get any insight to the answer.

Genesis 5:2 says, "He created them male and female, and He blessed *them* and named *them* Man [Adam] in the day when they were created" (emphasis added).

Did you ever see that God made *two* Adams in Genesis? Why did He do that? Because the word Adam means "man." God made two men; He made a female man and a mailman (guffaw). You say, "Well, that may be a great little item for the Bible Trivia

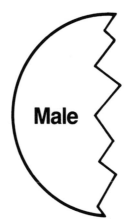

Figure 2.1

game, but what does that have to do with the subject?" Remember that we are trying to discern if one
or the other of these two people is basically superior. I
maintain that they are equal, but they have different
roles. God called them both "men" implying equality,
but later on He's going to establish different roles for
each of them.

So where did the name "woman" come from, my
sister? You got that from the guy God told to name
everything. Let's look at Genesis 2:23: "And the *man*
said, 'This is now bone of my bones, and flesh of my
flesh; She shall be called Woman . . . '" And God said,
"Okay, Woman it is." He's been calling you a woman
ever since, but originally you were called *man.*

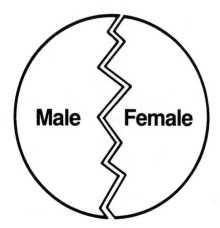

Figure 2.2

Let's look at another example to discern the original plan of equality.

> And God created man in His own image, in the image of God He created him; male and female He created them. And God blessed *them*; and God said to *them*, "Be fruitful and multiply, and fill the earth, and subdue it; and rule over the fish of the sea and over the birds . . . ." (Genesis 1:27-28, emphasis added)

God gave the marching orders to *them*, not to *him*. Try to be fruitful and multiply by yourself, guys. There is no evidence that the first man was out in front receiving the marching orders and the second "man" was peeking through the bushes saying, "What'd He say? What'd He say? Ask Him to speak up a little."

The plan is that we are one, gang. He has locked Anabel and me up in a little mini-lab with our toothbrushes in the same glass. The lab is designed for us to learn how to *agape* each other. Sure it's going to be tough at times. Without that it would be a snap, and we'd never be changed into His likeness through our experiences in the lab. But today's motto is, "When the going gets tough, get going to a lawyer." That's not the plan. That's a world-relief bail-out.

Now we certainly understand, after years of counseling, that there are extreme circumstances at times, such as physical abuse or child molestation, where separation should be considered. However, as God allows Satan to remove all *false* restraints (i.e., cultural taboos) in these last days, so that "only he who restrains" remains (2 Thessalonians 2:7), many Christians are divorcing merely because they are discontent in their marriage. This may temporarily relieve the pressure, but it will never conform them to the image of Christ.

ANABEL: Honey, before we go on, step over to the bookshelf and get *Shadows Over Stonewycke*. Share with them that part about commitment that is so good.

BILL: Yeah. Let's see, I believe it begins on page 169. Here it is . . .

"Your wife must love you very much."

"Of course! She is my wife."

"It does not necessarily follow that she must love you. Many wives stop loving their husbands."

"Ah, that shows how little you truly understand marriage. No wife ever stopped loving her husband, when he was truly loving *her* as a man was intended to love a woman."

"Are you saying people do not fall in love, and then out of it again?"

"What has falling in love to do with marriage? Nothing! You are not married, are you?"

"Actually, I am married."

"Then for your sake—and your wife's—I hope that someday soon you leave behind this foolishness about being 'in love.' No marriage can survive unless it gets past that and to the love of sacrifice. Ah, but you are young!"

"But you said your wife loved you. I assume you love her?"

"Of course! Of course! We are in love now because we first learned how to sacrifice ourselves one to the other. We have learned to serve, to lay down our lives, to wash each other's feet, so to speak. You don't do those kinds of things year after year unless you are determined to love. Not *in* love, but *determined* to love."

"I guess I always thought love had to come first in a marriage."

"No, my friend. Love—that comes second! First comes commitment, sacrifice. Then, and *only* then, comes *true* and lasting love. That is why my wife and I are *now* in love."

He said no more. He had certainly been given plenty to think about.†

---

† Adapted with permission from Michael Phillips and Judith Phillips, *Shadows Over Stonewycke* (Minneapolis: Bethany House Publishers, 1988).

3

HE MADE US DIFFERENT — BUT WHY?

A NABEL: Not long ago, I received this letter from a single woman . . .

Dear Anabel,

The Lord impressed me greatly with what you both said about our needs as men and women. I applied it to how I could meet the needs of my Christian brothers by esteeming them, deferring to them, respecting them, and not destroying or competing with them. It's exciting how much He is showing me in that area.

I am looking at it in a totally new way. Because I know I have a need to be loved and cared for and because I know how it destroys me when I'm not, I now see how it is a very real need for men to be respected and feel they can be leaned upon and praised. Before, I only saw it as a command to wives and husbands; but oh, the depths of our Lord's wisdom! It can work for me right now as a single woman seeking to be used in this way to meet my brothers' needs.

BILL: Anabel and I have developed a diagram of a model showing the needs of the husband and wife. The areas of the spirit, soul, and body are in contrasting shades. We're going to take a quick scan over this diagram and then elaborate in more detail later.

You'll notice by looking at the white portion of the diagram that Anabel and I are exactly the same in the area of the spirit. We each have an identical need. We need to *know* Jesus. But when we depart from the spirit area and move over into the soul, we're a different breed of cat.

Look at the emotions, the lightly shaded part. Honey, I need to *feel* like you're proud of me. I need you to praise me. How about you? What do you need?

ANABEL: I need TLC — tender loving care — and I'd like to elaborate on that just a tad.

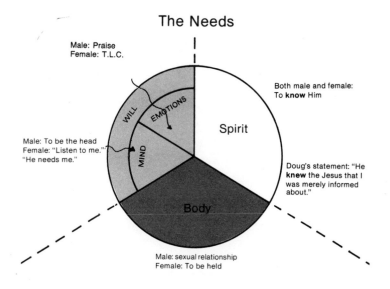

Figure 3.1

Tender communicates gentleness. I need you to be tender in your touch, yes, but it goes further than that. I need you to be tender in the way you look at me. Sometimes a husband's eyes will communicate anger or hostility or frustration. I also need you to watch the way you speak to me. Speak tenderly, please.

Loving means understanding (at least trying to understand) my thoughts—my behavior. It means recognizing my ability to do certain things and encouraging me to do them. It also means that you recognize my inability to do certain things and that you don't expect me to do them. It means remembering special days, and even more important, making very difficult and tedious days "special."

Care communicates respect. It means treating me as a person worthy of dignity and honor and letting others, especially my family and my children, see you caring for me in that way. It also communicates protection, protection that you would give to a very rare and precious gem. I need those things. They make me *feel* so special.

BILL: Moving on to another area of the soul, the mind. I need to *believe* something about our relationship, Honey. I need to believe in my mind that I am the head.

ANABEL: Why?

BILL: *Because God said so!* Naw . . . I was just kidding. I'd say that when you let me be the head, it gives me a sense of importance in our relationship; it enables me to believe I'm needed. It allows me to believe that you can't get along as well without me as you can with me. I *need* that. It enhances my sense of self-worth in our relationship. I need to believe I'm necessary.

ANABEL: I can see that, Honey, and I have those very same needs. I have this need for a sense of competency, for a feeling of self-worth, of importance in our relationship, to be needed. . . . I'll have all of those needs met if you will just *listen* to me.

BILL: Just listen to you? Put a number on that, Honey. How much do you need me to listen to you?

ANABEL: That's a ten.

BILL: I don't understand that. And hey, brother, don't you sit there and try to look smug like you *do* understand it. You're as in the dark as I am about what makes a woman tick. We've got to humble ourselves and listen to our wives if we're ever going to learn how to make our marriages fly. The irony of it all is that they can read us like the morning paper! We must listen to our wives so that we can learn how to love them like Jesus loves His wife, the Church (and that word "love" means far more than the "warm fuzzies").

Now, Hon, in the physical area, the body, I need a sexual relationship with my wife. What do you need?

ANABEL: Well, that's fine. Women enjoy that, too. But there are times when I don't want that at all. I just want to be held. It makes me feel secure.

BILL: Just hold you. And stop it right there.

ANABEL: Yes. You see, if every time I sit close to you on the divan, if every time I snuggle up to you, if every time you hold me, we wind up backing toward the bedroom, I get the impression that you're not interested in meeting *my* needs at all. You're just interested in getting *your* needs met. And do you know what I'll eventually do, Honey? Stop sitting close and stop snuggling up. Women frequently say to me, "Anabel, the only time my husband pays any attention to me is when he wants sex."

BILL: Put a number on how strongly you feel about this point you're making.

ANABEL: That's a ten. All of these are tens with me.

BILL: They're all tens? Hummmmm . . . Okay. Well, let's go back to the diagram and elaborate on each of these areas. We'll begin where we started, with our spirit. Honey, share with them what the Lord has shown us on just what it means to "know" Jesus. It goes far beyond salvation, doesn't it?

ANABEL: As Bill and I discussed this and tried to come up with something that would communicate "knowing Christ," we decided to share with you an experience that we had years ago when we were involved with the Lay Witness Mission movement.

When a church decides to have a Lay Witness Mission, the pastor will contact a coordinator. This man has a list of lay people who have committed themselves to devoting their weekends to this ministry. These folks, in turn, go to the host church in order to give their testimonies and to witness to the power of Christ in their lives.

We were on an LWM in Wichita Falls, Texas. The team had arrived early on Friday, and the coordinator was helping us get acquainted with other team members. He pointed to the back of the room and said, "Doug, come up here and share your testimony with the team." This very impressive gentleman stood up and came to the front of the room. He was impeccably dressed — a handsome man.

He began to share with us. "My name is Doug. I'm very wealthy, so much so that I became bored with taking care of all my assets and hired someone to do that for me. I decided to pursue something else in life. I went back to school and got my doctor's degree in biology, then became a professor at a university here in Texas."

"Well, soon that became boring to me, and I determined to pursue something else in life, so I decided to become a Christian. I went to the library and read a lot of books on the subject. I then aligned myself with a local church, and because of my prestige in the community, I was immediately placed on many important boards. It was no surprise to me when the pastor called one day and said, 'Doug, we're going to conduct a Lay Witness Mission in our church. Would you chair the committee to prepare for the team's visit?' And, as a matter of course, I said I would."

Doug did a super job in preparation, as you can imagine, and now the weekend had arrived when all of these lay people were converging on their church. On Friday night, the church members divided up into small groups of eight or ten people, and one of the laywitnesses went with a group to a secluded little room to tell of his relationship with Christ. Doug, along with several other members of his church, was assigned to a small group. I'll let him pick up the story again. . . .

"As we were walking back to our assigned room, I began to evaluate the young man who was going to be sharing with us. He was very obviously a common, laboring man. He even had oil under his fingernails like he might have been a mechanic or something. I began to think, 'I really should be in charge of this group. I am quite sure that I could handle it much more effectively than he could.'"

They got to their room, they sat down, and the young man began to share. Doug said this:

"As he began to share about his relationship with Christ, I became intensely aware of something: That young man *knew* the Jesus that I was merely informed about."

My dear brother, my dear sister, I have got to *know* Him—and so does Bill. Information will not suffice when deep waters threaten all you hold dear. The Scriptures do not say, "*If* you pass through deep waters," but "*when* you pass through deep waters" (Isaiah 43:2, emphasis added). They come to each of us. We do not come to you out of a vacuum. We don't sit in an ivory tower. We have had many "trials and tribulations," but in them all and through them all we have come to *know* the sufficiency of the Lord. A.W. Tozer says that after the initial experience of salvation, there comes "the glorious pursuit of knowing Him."

BILL: One of my heroes is Hosea; he's going to be one of the first people I hug when I get to heaven, because God has used him in my life to demonstrate

Christ's faithfulness to the Church as His beloved Bride.

Hosea typifies God's relationship to Israel, but remember that you and I are spiritual Israel (Galatians 3:29; Romans 9:6-8), so this story is a typology of Jesus' relationship to us.

Hosea's unfaithful wife, Gomer, had a near zero commitment to her husband, but he kept pursuing her, loving her, forgiving her, picking up the pieces of her unfaithfulness towards him. Then, in chapters 1 and 2, the book of Hosea shows how Christ patiently leads us through deep, deep waters until He is all we have left. Someone has said that most of us never discover that Christ is all we *need* until He is all we *have*. Deep water does that for you.

Through Gomer's experience, we discern that we must come to the end of ourselves if we are ever to make a marvelous discovery: Jesus is not a burdensome taskmaster to us, but a loving Husband.

> "And it will come about in *that* day [the deepwater day]," declares the Lord, "that you will call Me Ishi [my Husband] and will no longer call Me Baali [my Master]. (Hosea 2:16, emphasis added)

> "And I will betroth you to Me forever; Yes, I will betroth you to Me in righteousness and in justice, in lovingkindness and in compassion, and I will betroth you to Me in faithfulness. *Then* you will *know* the Lord." (Hosea 2:19-20, emphasis added)

ANABEL: I love Philippians 3:10-11 in the Amplified translation:

[For my determined purpose is] that I may *know* Him—that I may progressively become more deeply and intimately acquainted with Him, perceiving and recognizing and understanding [the wonders of His person] more strongly and more clearly. And that I may, in that same way, come to *know* the power outflowing from His resurrection [which it exerts over believers]; and that I may so share His sufferings as to be continually transformed [in spirit into His likeness even] to His death, [in the hope] that if possible, I may attain to the [spiritual and moral] resurrection [that lifts me] out from among the dead [even while in the body]. (emphasis added)

BILL: That's Paul's life-verse, isn't it? We all need that regardless of our gender, don't we Hon?

ANABEL: Yes. The truths explained in your book, *Lifetime Guarantee*, are a valuable tool in satisfying this need we have to know Him.

BILL: Okay, let's move into the area of the soul. Whereas Anabel and I are identical in the spirit, from here on we're different. If we weren't, how could we ever complete one another? So, Sugar, in the area of the emotions, I need to *feel* like you are proud of me. I need you to praise me. Now, how do we know that? Quote that verse for them that says you're supposed to praise me. And quote it out of the Amplified translation because it's so much longer in that one. It drags it way out with lots and lots of verbs.

ANABEL:

. . . And let the wife see that she respects and reverences her husband — that she notices him, regards him, honors him, prefers him, venerates and esteems him; and that she defers to him, praises him, and loves and admires him exceedingly. (Ephesians 5:33b, Amplified)

BILL: I love it. What a marvelous truth from God's Word! I have asked Anabel to sew it onto some cloth and frame it for me, but she seems never to have enough time to get around to it. (Smile.)

I *need* female praise. I don't need flattery. The Bible says that "Flattery is a form of hatred and wounds cruelly" (Proverbs 26:28 TLB). It's not that I have an ego problem. God created us males with this need for female praise. We were born with it just as females were born with a need for male TLC.

Let me illustrate. Here's a little kid six years old. He's hanging by his heels from a limb in the apple tree in his back yard. Who does he yell at to come out and see him? Mom! "Hey, Mom! C'mere!" See? He's trying to show the main female in his life what a stud he is. *He can do a physical, masculine thing that "his" female can't do.* If she steps to the door and says, "Wow . . . how can you stay up there like that? Aren't you afraid you'll fall?", it thrills him to death. We males love that sort of thing. It makes us *feel* male.

ANABEL: What would happen, Honey, if I were his mom and decided to go out and demonstrate my expertise as a "tree-hanger" and out-performed him?

BILL: Well, I doubt that he could verbalize his feelings at that age, and individual differences being as they are, one might be disappointed at being bested by "his woman" and lose interest in climbing trees, whereas another might grit his teeth and vow he'd learn to hang by one foot in order to outdo you.

Now let's look in on him at age ten or so. He's weaning himself off of Mom, and he's getting more into the ten-year-old women. He can't hang in the tree and holler, "Hey girls, look!" That'd be uncool. So what you do is get all set hanging in the tree when you see them coming down the street and as they pass by, you make a lot of noise. Then you imagine they're thinking the same thoughts your Mom used to verbalize to you . . . "Wow, look at that!" And you get that same good *feeling* that you're a stud.

Let's have him grow up some more and put him in high school. This whole process gets more sophisticated as we mature, so tree-hanging is out. High school women just aren't really that impressed with hanging from trees. You've got to do something more spectacular, like be an athlete. You sweat blood out there, and when you finally get your letter jacket, you practice looking cool in front of the mirror; then you practice walking cool, and when you get all this down pat, you stroll down the halls of the high school and bask in the admiring glances of the girls. Hey, that's what pompon girls are all about! The girls know it's a game and so do the guys. We've all played it, right?

It's the way God made us. Hey, when the camera zooms in on the guy who scored in an NFL game, what does he say? "Hi, Mom!" I know he's putting us on, but he doesn't say, "Hi, Dad," does he? We males need female praise, and that's a ten.

ANABEL: That reminds me of a pertinent story. I was sunning myself at a swimming pool, and two young couples were the only other people there. Apparently, one couple had a pretty comfortable relationship, but the other kids were just becoming acquainted.

The boy went over to the diving board and called to his girlfriend to come with him. She was a cute little thing. She slid into the pool and swam over. He perched on the end of the board and kept bouncing, waiting until all eyes were on him before he began his exhibition. I even heard him mumble under his breath, "You all better watch me." Finally he dived in, giving a passing fair performance.

Then the girl climbed out of the pool and onto the board where she poised on her toes for a moment and then executed a beautiful dive, hardly making a splash as her slender body entered the water.

As they climbed out of the pool together, I heard the guy say, "Let's go play some basketball. . . ."

BILL: Yeah, sometimes there's a lot of ham in us, Sugar, when it comes to needing our special woman to see us as manly.

I'm going to give Anabel a ten on this one. She has always given me praise, even during those years when I was giving her such misery. It's really been amazing. Let me share a couple of anecdotes to illustrate.

One night I was up late reading and Anabel was already in bed. I tried to be as quiet as possible as I slipped into my side and eased the covers up, not wanting to disturb her. But she was awake. She reached over, patted me on the hip and said, "I'm so proud you're my husband." You talk about feeling ten feet tall. To have that sweet thing say things like that to me makes me feel like a king.

Here's another one. One time a man offered to let our family use his vacation cottage up on Lake Superior in Canada for a two-week vacation and, naturally, I *felt led* to accept it. God wants all His children to vacation in Canada, right? So, we went up there, and Anabel was sitting out on the deck doing her needle work. Her thimble slipped off her finger, dropped through a crack in the boards, and went into the lake. She went into the cabin, rummaged around until she found another thimble, and went back to her sewing again. This time I was sitting out there on the deck with her. The thimble came off again, hit on her leg and was heading for the water. I reached out from my chaise lounge, picked the thimble out of the air and handed it back to her. She said, "Your coordination just amazes me. . . ." Hey, I love that kind of stuff!

I was telling this story in one of our live seminars out at Forest Home Conference Center in California one time, and at the break a man came up to me and said, "Man, if my wife would say things like that to me, I'd dive in after that other thimble!"

On the other hand, some guys can't relate to these examples. When I talk to them about needing their wife's praise, thoughts come into their mind like, "Well, I wouldn't want my wife to tell me I was coordinated. Now, Gillham is different. He seems like sort of a sissy anyway. He probably goes for that, but I don't."

Those thoughts are not being generated in his "sound mind"; they're being *served up* to his mind by the power of sin. They're coming to him with *first person singular pronouns* (I, me) as Sgt. Sin capitalizes on his stuck feeler! He's never been able to receive praise because he doesn't *feel* worthy of it. His *feeler's stuck.*

Somehow in childhood, this dear man learned to consider himself unworthy of praise. If he ever received any, he *felt* unworthy of it, or *felt* uncomfortable in hearing it, or *felt* like the giver was a phony or was undiscerning. Now that he's saved, Sgt. Sin (the devil's agent) works continually through his flesh to block him from being able to receive the praise from his wife that God intends him to have. He is being blocked by his stuck feeler. His solution lies in understanding how to appropriate his true identity in Christ.

ANABEL: Someone has equated the emotion that a woman will experience when her husband is having an affair to the emotion a man will experience when his wife refuses to praise him.

You might say, "No way do those compare, Anabel." Oh, but they do. You see, when my husband seeks out another woman, what he is essentially saying to me is this: "Your femininity is simply not pleasing to me. I am going to find someone whose femininity pleases me." And what I am saying to my husband when I do not praise him is, "Sorry, but your masculinity just is not pleasing to me. Quite frankly, I see nothing in you to praise."

One time we were doing our seminar in Georgia, and a lady wrote this note to me; I asked her permission to share it.

> I sat in the seminar listening as though you were speaking directly to me as you spoke of the "strong woman." I am a strong woman. I was raised by my divorced mother who was the epitome of independence and strength. Need a man? Ha! Boy, that was not part of the program. Need a man to make a decision? Are you kidding? I am an independent, strong-willed performer, though I don't look it. I'm 5'2", 105 lbs. But I have a will of iron, and it is ruin-

ing my life. There is a constant *power struggle* between my husband and myself.

I'm saved and I've read the scriptures, but they did not sink in. God spoke to me last night when you said someone compared the emotions a woman has (knowing her husband has had an affair) to the emotions a man has when he does not get praise from his wife. I could not believe my ears! You see, I never praise my husband. I always think: "He can't make a decision that is right."

Last night I had a dream. I dreamed that my husband had an affair. And I mean I dreamed the *details*. I actually *felt* the emotions as if it were true. It hurt so badly! I woke up at 4:30 A.M. sobbing. At that point I realized what I was doing! Anabel, this was God's work in me!

I guess one of the most vivid illustrations of this happened in one of our counseling sessions. We were talking with a couple who had been married for thirteen years. They were together in the room, and at the height of the man's tirade, he turned to his wife — with all of the vehemence he could muster — with all of the hostility built through the years — and he said to her, "Never, my *dear* wife, never in thirteen long years of marriage did you *ever* praise me in front of anyone!"

And you are prone to mutter, "Big deal. Bless his poor, little heart." Yes, bless his heart, because you see, God has placed a need in my husband — a need for female praise. And He has given me to my husband to meet that need.

BILL: That's right on target, Hon. And you know, it breaks my heart to hear one of my sisters in Christ make disparaging remarks to her kids about their dad's qualifications as the leader of the family. I just ache for the poor guy, imagining what it would be like were I in his shoes. You can never know, Sugar, how many times I thank God for giving me a woman who would never undermine me like that with my sons.

ANABEL: During a seminar in California, a man came up to me and said, "Anabel, may I talk to you for a minute?" He was an older gentleman, and it was interesting to me that he was holding a hat in his hands and would twist it as he talked.

We isolated ourselves and he began. "Anabel, you know the story you told about the man whose wife did not praise him for thirteen years?"

"Yes," I said.

He looked down at his hat, twisted it a little and when he looked up, his eyes were tear-filled. He quickly looked back down, regained his composure and then said, "Would you believe thirty-nine years, Anabel?"

"I beg your pardon?"

"Yes. Thirty-nine *long* years. I'm damned if I do, and I'm damned if I don't."

BILL: But, Honey, wouldn't she be a phony if she began to praise her husband, and she didn't *feel* that he was worthy of it? Wouldn't that make her a hypocrite?

ANABEL: That's why our introduction summarizes the teaching from your book, *Lifetime Guarantee.* You can go to a seminar on marriage and come home with your arms loaded with books and your brain loaded with good intentions, but instead of becoming the "Total Woman," in two weeks you're the "totalled" woman. You simply can't do it unless you know how to trust Christ to do it all for you, through you.

I have had women rather irately say to me, "Look, Anabel. I'm not playing games. My husband is a loser, a real loser. I'm not going to make up things to praise him for."

And I have to explain to her, "My dear sister. You are not 'playing games;' you are being obedient. You won't be 'making up' things to praise him for; you'll be trusting the Holy Spirit within you to show them to you. They'll be valid things, not flattery. You will be meeting a need, a God-given need, for your husband."

BILL: Our son, Pres, makes the following statement in his teaching: "Encouragement should be for small things as well as larger things. It should not be limited to performance tasks that are well done. Characteristics, attributes, desires, and admirable qualities are good objects for encouragement as well. This perspective will act to build up the person for who he *is* as opposed to what he has done."

ANABEL: I love Ken Taylor's paraphrase of the Proverbs. Let me share some of them with you that emphasize the husband's need to feel that his wife is proud of him. "A nagging wife annoys like constant dripping. A father can give his sons homes and riches, but only the Lord can give them understanding wives" (Proverbs 19:13b-14). "A worthy wife is her husband's joy and crown" (Proverbs 12:4a).

By my behavior, I can become a "crown" for my husband:

1. My children see him as king.

2. The people around me see him as king.

3. I bestow on him all of the rights, responsibilities, and honors of a king.

4. He will see himself as king.

Thus, he is secure in that position. He is not threatened; and because of this, he is neither forced to overly compensate by being domineering or sarcastic nor is he forced to abdicate his role because of a lack of confidence. A wife becomes her husband's crown through her attitude, her behavior, and her interaction with him and everyone else in the house.

Let's go on with the verses from Proverbs; remember, "a worthy wife is her husband's joy and crown." (Now listen carefully to this.) "The other kind corrodes his strength and tears down everything he does" (12:4b). "It is better to live in the corner of an attic than with a crabby woman in a lovely home" (21:9). "Better to live in the desert than with a quarrelsome, complaining woman" (21:19). A wife can either encourage her husband as he assumes his God-given role, or fight him for it and assume it herself.

There is no way that I can do what is required of me in my marriage. But as I allow Jesus Christ, who indwells me and who is now my very Life (Colossians 3:4) to perform through me, He will meet this need in my husband — beautifully! Oh, please listen. There is such victory available to you as you apply the truth of our true identity in Christ to your marriage. He wants to do it all *for* you, through you, but you must cooperate with Him in order to experience it. You must choose the way of the cross and offer yourself as a living sacrifice through which Christ can minister to your husband.

4

A MALE'S NEED— NOT HIS RIGHT

*B*ILL: This letter from our files is pretty typical of what I hear from many husbands.

Bill:

Pat and I have been separated now since March 23rd. We see each other about once a week, but we don't get much accomplished. From my point of view, she builds my hate and resentment towards her by being so "bossy." It seems like she's on my back constantly about how I'm failing, and I just take it and take it; then finally, before I do something that I know I'll be sorry for later, I leave.

She says she lost respect for me because I didn't make decisions, but when I did, she would not go along with them unless they were identical to what she wanted to do or what she thought ought to be done. She would either ridicule me or run me down. If it was really important, she would lose her temper and tear something up.

How, as I've asked her so many times, do you win in a situation like that? Maybe I went about making decisions in the wrong way, maybe I was too dogmatic or something. But I simply don't understand how to deal with her.

That man's letter makes it clear, Honey. We husbands need to *believe* something about our relationship. We need to believe that we're the head of it.

But boy, have we males blown it by the ways we've tried to get you gals to submit to our leadership! Too often we've had the attitude, "Male redbirds are prettier than female redbirds; I'm bigger than you are; I can throw a rock straighter than you can; I know which way is north; therefore, you ought to recognize me as your authority." That goes over like a lead balloon with our wives, and no small wonder!

Consider the man who is the head of a firm and has employees with various job descriptions. To what extent will that man go in order to ensure a successful company with a loyal, contented, and productive work force? What would some of his leadership responsibilities include?

- Establish safe and efficient working conditions

- Use sound, motivational techniques

- Provide health care

- Establish good relationships with employees

- Be mindful of the emotional needs of each employee

- Provide vacation time

- Delegate duties within the bounds of the job descriptions

- Practice constructive criticism

- Be consistent as a leader of integrity and fair treatment

Should the head of the firm incorporate all of these qualities and responsibilities into his leadership style, he would never need to demand, manipulate, or threaten any of his employees. Rather, a general desire to do the very best possible would pervade the work force.

Now with regard to the husband's leadership: If the husband, in his role as head, does not demand like some fanatical autocrat, "You submit to my authority," "You do as I say," "You do not question the decision that I set forth," etc., but rather fulfills his responsibilities as leader of the family, then the results will be the same: partnership, compatibility, unity, loyalty, and respect from his wife.

Whereas I gave Anabel a 10 on praising me, I'm not going to give her a 10 on this one. Her lack of submission to my headship and my subsequent domineering attempts to control her caused us to experience, as Anabel says, "That blissful state of marriage called 'hell on earth.'" Anabel has forgiven me for coming across like that for so many years. Hon, I *need* for you to see me as a man with a void that only you can optimally fill. I *need* to be your head. God created me this way. It isn't that I'm such a red-hot leader or that I'm on a big ego trip, but that I've got to be the head of something . . . and you're elected.

ANABEL: Gee, thanks.

BILL: Just because I was created by our Father to be the head doesn't mean that I am any better than you. It's just that we were created with different roles to "life out" on Planet Earth. You and I are to fit together as one and to do that we must have different needs which mesh, right?

ANABEL: Yes. It has taken the sting out of submitting to you as my head by seeing in Scripture that I am your equal. Our relationship is the same as Jesus' is to the Father. Jesus is the Father's equal, but He totally submits to the Father's authority over Him (see Philippians 2:6 and 1 Corinthians 15:28). They're equal, but They each have different roles in Their relationship.

Some wives choose to resist their God-ordained role and try to control their husbands. The following is an excerpt from a letter we received from a husband which illustrates the point clearly:

> It's a vicious circle! Janice runs our house, but doesn't really want to. It's impossible to satisfy her! Her need for precision and order is never ending, and my ability to perform at all levels is inconsistent according to *her* standards. She then believes that our relationship is unbalanced and doesn't feel capable of giving me the things I desperately need at that particular time. I start to feel rejected and unacceptable to her as a husband and father and wind up seeking acceptance somewhere else . . . in the arms of another woman. I hate it, but I simply don't know how to change things.

BILL: I remember a couple I saw years ago. They were both born-again, but when the guy confessed that he'd had eleven affairs, they decided it was time to come in for counseling.

One day she was coming to see me alone and was late arriving, explaining that her car wouldn't start. Then she said, "So I raised the hood, removed the breather, freed up the automatic choke, put the breather back on, and it kicked right off."

I said, "You're kidding!"

She said, "Oh, no. When anything goes wrong, I fix it. Last week the element burned out in my oven. I flipped the breaker off and removed the element, went to the electric shop and bought a replacement, installed it, turned the breaker on and was back in business. Why, if I waited around for that louse to fix things they never would get done."

I said, "You're not going to like what I've got to tell you. I agree that your husband has blown it royally, but you are a major part of the problem. By usurping his role, you are making him feel that he's unnecessary. Your strength makes him believe you can get along better without him than you can with him." In fact, when emotions were high around the house, that's precisely what she and their daughter would scream at him. Guess what the major problem will most likely be in the daughter's marriage.

Of course, the guy was guilty eighteen ways from Sunday (eleven actually) for what he had done. I'm not minimizing that, but we're dealing with the male's needs. We'll get to the female's later on, so bear with us. The guy was out there in those foreign beds trying to *feel* like he was indeed attractive and necessary to a woman. Sinning? Yes. Excusable? Certainly not. Accountable for his sinning? Yes. But understand, dear people, what was motivating the man and how Satan was capitalizing on it.

ANABEL: *Home* to some men means insecurity — to others failure — to others bedlam — or hostility — or pressure — rejection of what they say — rejection of what they do — rejection of who they are; and the role that we as wives play in our husbands' images of home cannot be overemphasized.

BILL: I took two years of shop in high school and came out with a billy club and a little gun rack; not too swift, but at about age thirty or so, I began to believe that I could make things out of wood. That's macho, so I was kind of eager to give it another try. Success would feed my masculine needs.

I bought a saber saw and some wood and whipped out a little shelf. I gave it to Anabel, and we hung it on the wall and put her little trinkets on it. When company came over, she'd say, "Look what my smart husband did." I'd try to act cool, but inside I was loving it. So, I became a prolific shelf-maker. They're all over our house now.

I milked that deal till it ran dry and then retired from shelf-making. You know, you can never satisfy the flesh, and I was doing all of this to get *my* need for masculine self-esteem met, not to make shelves for Anabel.

The years went by, and one day Anabel came to me and said, "Honey, I need you to make another shelf for the boys' room." Delbert Dumb here didn't realize she was saying, "Husband, love me one more time like you used to." I thought she was asking me to make a shelf, and I had no motivation to make more shelves. I'd already done that, and it didn't excite me now. I ignored her. A month went by, and she asked me again. I ignored her. Another month, another request. I ignored her.

Then one day I came home from the office and she said, "Hi, Honey. I've got a surprise for you today!" She took me by the hand, led me back to the boys' room, and there on the wall was a new shelf that she had made, and it looked as good as mine. Something died in me when I saw that shelf. I don't recall how I responded; I probably remarked that it looked nice, but I was downcast inside. Years later as I was counseling, the Lord brought that episode to mind, and I understood what had happened to me. When I saw that shelf, it made me feel like Anabel could get along just fine without me, that she didn't really need me.

Sweet sister, did God raise you up as a new woman in Christ who was strong as an acre of garlic? No, you are the product of a "planned pregnancy," and you were reborn to submit to your hubby. Okay, so where did your assertive strength come from? It's a do-it-yourself job; perhaps you *had* to be strong in order to survive, so you developed it. Perhaps you were reared by strong people, and the key to their acceptance and to self-acceptance was to be strong, so you accomplished it by playing "lord of the ring." It's all "flesh" now.

Please listen . . . If you are my sister in Christ and you have strong flesh, you are probably not married to a guy who is stronger than you, but to a man with passive flesh or with macho flesh. If it is the former and you're twenty years into your marriage, your constant prayer is, "Lord, dynamite this guy off the divan and get him involved in this home. He just sits there and says, 'Go ask your mom.'" If it's the latter, then there is probably a hot war on land, sea, and in the air. He may be insulting you with cutting remarks in front of your friends, family, and even the check-out clerks. You are the subject of open ridicule, or at best, sarcastic wit. There may have been affairs over the years, and your husband may even be one of the super stars in the church. How do I know? Because that describes Bill and Anabel (with the exception of the affairs). But, praise God, He has turned things around through the truths we are describing in this book.

If you are married to a threatened male, don't compete with him and beat the daylights out of him in ping-pong, badminton, and croquet. He'll take up winter camping — above timberline. He will freeze you out. He'll be forced to try to accomplish some macho thing you can't beat him at. Don't kill him in bridge, hearts, and pitch in front of your friends, or he'll take up stamp collecting and insist you go to the parties without him.

This is a response from husbands that just breaks our hearts: "Don't compete with me in your Christianity, or I'll quit going to church with you. You attend two Bible studies each week; you've got your memory verses stuck all over the house; you've got five Bibles — all underlined — and one lying open on the coffee table hoping I'll read it. I hear you talking to your prayer partner on the phone, and you sound like a King James Bible. You use words like 'quicken' and 'tarry.' Hey, nobody says tarry any more! We make bathrobes out of that stuff! Becoming a Christian while living with you scares me to death." If this is your husband, and he ever *does* get saved, he'll be a closet-Christian until you eject from your earthsuit. He's not going to get into one more environment with you where he has to begin on a bicycle, and you're already in a Mercedes loaded with gas.

If your strength is your darling security, you may think you'd die if you were to lose it; but it's precisely the thing the Holy Spirit is trying to put to death in order that Christ might *become* your strength. Will you swap your strength for His Life through you? Tell Him you desire that. The refining process won't be easy, but you'll love the results.

ANABEL: Let me ask you a question here, Honey. You've shared with us about your folks. Your mom was very definitely the leader. But if we could have talked with them about their "upside-down relationship," I daresay Mom would have said, "But I enjoy taking the lead. I have always been a forceful, aggressive, competent person. I don't mind the role of leader. I'm very comfortable with it." And if you could have talked to Pop, he would have said, "Oh, she likes to make decisions and confront people. I don't. She's always made the decisions around here, and I like it that way." Tell me, Honey, why should a couple change if they like it? They're both comfortable in their roles. Why make waves?

BILL: We're back to the law of gravity again. When a marriage is set up so that the wife is "lifing out" the role of husband by being the authority figure and the husband is "lifing out" the role of wife by submitting to his wife's authority, then something is going to go splat. Something will suffer, be it the marriage, the kids, the grandkids, or whatever, because you don't violate God's ways without experiencing problems. He's God. The neat thing is that *His* ways are all for *our* good (see Romans 8:28-29).

ANABEL: I guess one of the best ways to communicate this point is to allow a wife who has experienced it to talk to us about it. The following letter from a friend is a dramatic illustration of this type of marriage and its subsequent result in this dear person's being transferred, against her will, to the single-again group:

Dear Anabel,

Do we ever fit the former Gillham family portrait. What an unbelievable mess. Hell on earth created so quietly under a roof in a house that appeared to be a home to the world looking in.

One of our biggies has been competition. I have beaten him in every physical activity we have ever participated in. I took up bicycling a couple of years ago and worked at it diligently. A two-hundred-mile-ride in two days was a recreational trek! I'd think he was a real cream puff because he couldn't whip off twenty-five miles (just a stroll for me) without being worn out.

Tennis? Oh, yes. I could wipe him off the court. I practiced diligently, took lessons, and had a lot of natural ability. I couldn't wait to get him on the court and show him how good I was.

Last year we got a twenty-five foot sailboat. He had dreamed of this boat and spent months reading how to maneuver and sail it. You know, it takes a bit of expertise to put it in the slip without scraping the sides or bumping the bow. Well, guess who qualified as an expert . . . first try? I did do one thing smart, Anabel. I never tried to sail it while he was on board. I've really proven myself in many areas; unfortunately, none of them encouraged my husband to want to spend any "fun" time with me.

We went to see them as quickly as we could and talked with her first. She realized what had happened and wanted the chance to try again *so* badly. Then we went to see him. We weren't quite sure about his address, so he met us at a designated parking lot—in his Porsche. We followed him to his very nice bachelor pad. He took off his suit coat, loosened his tie, and offered us refreshments. As we began talking he listened very politely, and when we had finished, he said to us, "You've no idea how I appreciate your love and your interest, but I have no intention of getting back in the marriage, no intention at all." Then he paused . . . we waited. He finally spoke, "But if I ever should, I'd win next time." How heartbreaking.

So many stories — from real people. I think of a meeting we attended as conferees. One of the most attractive couples at the conference wound up sitting with us in a relaxed atmosphere. He was a very successful businessman — she was a very successful businesswoman. He talked about his clients, and she talked about her clients. They seemed to complement each other so nicely.

One morning before the conference ended there was a knock at our hotel door. It was the husband, and we asked him in. Before we could start any small talk, he blurted out, "I'm leaving my wife."

We looked at each other, then at him and said, "What in the world?"

I never shall forget his answer: "Mary doesn't *need* me. She will do just fine without me. I have found a woman who needs me."

BILL: This is so common today. How subtly the enemy is eroding the home. I'm sure you have seen "The Cosby Show"; in it, the Huxtable males are portrayed as laid-back, jovial, and easy-going while the females are depicted as aggressive and assertive. In a head-to-head conflict over a major family issue between the females and the males in their household, who would you put your money on?

ANABEL: How many files do we have — files with tragic stories caged inside — of cases where a man has left a very efficient, capable, independent, strong-willed woman for "a woman who needs me"?

It isn't that a man falls out of love with one woman and in love with another, but that he finds frustration with one and fulfillment with another . . . and he calls it *love*.

BILL: In reality, it's just that his needs are being met. Listen carefully, we have come to believe, after counseling many hundreds of couples, that the marriage most vulnerable to divorce is one in which either a passive or a macho husband is in union with a wife who comes on too strong. The only surefire, guaranteed way to defuse such a "self-destruct marriage" is for both parties to come to the end of their flesh trips and allow Christ to express His Life through them in order to meet one another's needs. Otherwise, it's just a matter of time until the marriage begins either to explode or implode.

ANABEL: Honey, let's talk about the "decision-making" process. That seems to be an area of great discussion, or should I say dissension? I've had some pretty difficult struggles with this, especially when I saw you making a decision for the family that I felt strongly was not the right one. Could you share how we have solved this problem and how the Lord has made you sensitive to my part in this aspect of our relationship?

BILL: In Figure 4:1, the left side represents the husband and the right the wife. Remember that each one is equipped with certain talents, abilities, and gifts by the One who created them. His goal is that they learn, under His authority over them, how to *agape* one another by faith.

Let's say Anabel and I are faced with the question, "Should we plant a big garden this spring?" Generally speaking, as a male I approach decisions from a logical perspective, whereas Anabel (female) approaches them intuitively. I might say, "Here are my reasons for

Figure 4.1

believing we should plant a big garden: A, B, C, etc."
Anabel, on the other hand, might say, "Well, I just
don't feel we should plant a garden this year"; and
when I ask why, she'd be hardpressed to give me seven
logical reasons why she feels the way she does.

For a long time, guys, I wrote her ideas off as illogical, but finally the Lord got it through my thick skull
that Anabel is not illogical, she's *intuitive* . . . and that
is excellent! She is the main source of intuitive input
in our relationship, and if I cut her off, *I'm* the one
who is being illogical. I'm cutting off my nose to spite
my face. God will speak to me through her if I'll just
listen. It's amazing, guys, how often you can share
problems with your wife in areas that she doesn't
know anything about, and God will give you solutions
through her just because you humble yourself to listen.

The Lord taught me this right after I entered the
counseling ministry. I had resigned my job as a
psychology professor in Oklahoma and had moved my
family to Springfield, Missouri, in order to direct an
office. For many weeks, my appointment calendar was
clean as a whistle. It was tough; one payday I got fifty-
nine dollars.

During these lean months, I began to sense that
God wanted Anabel to begin a women's Bible study,
and she agreed. We put a small ad in the paper inviting women to come to our home the following
Thursday morning, and forty-seven showed up! Our
house wouldn't hold that crowd, so they moved to a

larger house. The next week, as I recall, seventy-five came. The larger house wouldn't hold that crowd, so they rented a hall for the next week. The Saturday after that I was washing dishes (loving Anabel) and talking to the Lord. "Lord . . . I don't understand all this. All these women coming to hear Anabel teach the Bible . . . I can't even get 'em to come to me one at a time, and I'm the one You sent to Springfield, not Anabel! I'm not trying to get smart with You. I'm a broken man, and if You want me to be in a tiny ministry, that's just fine. I don't need the big crowd, but I sure would appreciate it if You'd explain what is happening."

Thoughts began to come to mind, and by faith, I believe this was the Lord responding to me. "Bill, you really admire Anabel, don't you?"

I said, "Yessir, I do. She's a very competent person."

He said, "Tell Me, Bill, aren't you and Anabel one?"

"Yessir."

"And you've always wanted to be a walking Bible concordance, like she is, haven't you?"

I said, "Yessir, I have."

"Well, congratulations. Now you are."

Do you see what He told me? God said that jagged line in Figure 4.1 doesn't exist. Anabel and I are like a cue ball on a snooker table. We are literally *one!* You say, "Oh, Bill, you're taking that too literally; it's just that God *sees* you as one." Right. I'll buy that. If God sees us as one, what are we? One.

Hey, I'm free! I don't have to compete with this hard-charger anymore! Whatever she can do, I am doing; whatever I can do, she's doing. We are one. We're in this thing together!

So, Honey, let's apply this oneness to the decision-making process. You and I have discussed the garden problem; we've prayed about it, and finally I say to you, "Well, Shug, I've come to a decision on this, and we're going to go ahead with the garden." Now what do I *not* need from you?

ANABEL: Before I answer that, I want to emphasize one point. We *did* discuss this, and you did *listen to me?*

BILL: Yes.

ANABEL: I mean that you gave me eye contact. You weren't leafing through the pages of the seed catalog and saying, "I'm listening, I'm listening. Go ahead with whatever it was you wanted to say." You didn't do that to me, did you?

BILL: No.

ANABEL: Okay, now, what is it you do *not* need from me once you come to me and say, "I've prayed about it, and I believe the Lord is telling me to plant a big garden . . ." Oh, perhaps something like this: "That's strange; I prayed about it too, and that certainly isn't the answer that I received from the Lord. I don't think we're to plant a big garden at all."

BILL: That would eat my lunch . . . really devastate me. So what is it that I *do* need you to say when I tell you I have my answer from the Lord?

ANABEL: You need me to encourage you, to support you, to reassure you. For example, "All right, what shall we plant? If we can decide now, I'll run down to the hardware store and get the seeds this afternoon."

BILL: Right . . . Wow, Honey, that makes me feel good. So three months later, after one of the biggest droughts in the history of Texas, we're sitting at the breakfast table, and the man on the radio says, "Well folks, it looks like another hot, dry week coming up." Let's say the boys are still young, and all six of us are at the table. What do I *not* need from you?

ANABEL: It could be very overt and cruel, designed deliberately to make you look bad in front of the boys: "Have you been out to see the garden lately, guys? We've labeled it 'Gillham's Folly.' One of these days your dad will learn to listen to me — but oh, no! He *had* to have his garden. With the money we've spent on that little project, I could have gone to the grocery store and bought fresh vegetables for the next two years!" Or it could be very covert: "What did the weatherman say today? I, uh, didn't hear it."

BILL: Here's where Sgt. Sin is going to speak to me with an Okie accent and first person pronouns to try to get me to react to your assault on my credibility. If I have macho flesh, Sgt. Sin will give me thought responses like, "Shut up! I told you to *shut up* about that garden, and now I'm telling you for the last time!" I'd be seething with feelings of hatred and revenge because you'd emasculated me in front of my sons.

But if I have passive flesh, Sgt. Sin will put thoughts into my mind like this, "Why? Why did I ever mention planting a garden? Oh Lord, if You'll ever let this pass away and be forgotten, I'll be so grateful to You. When will I learn that I *never* have good ideas, that she's *always* right. Oh, if only I were different, but I'll never change." Then I'd fade to black.

That passivity is flesh, not spirit, just as surely as dominance (whether male or female) is flesh. It is developed from day one, since infancy. The passive-flesh person has sought the goals of human acceptance and getting his needs for security and comfort satisfied through *weakness* in much the same manner as a puppy that tucks its tail and rolls over on its back. Sgt. Sin controls this man with either self-justifying or self-abasing thoughts; that is, any thoughts which will justify his staying away from where the action is or from where personal accountability is essential.

Honey, it's more obvious what might be taking place in the boys if I had macho-flesh outbursts, but how might they react if I had passive flesh and gave in to it like this?

ANABEL: Oh! It's horrible to think about. There may be one of them who's getting thoughts something like this, "Boy! My wife will never talk to me that way — I'll punch her out if she tries. I'd like to see Dad flatten her when she smarts off like that." He'd lose all respect for you as a father and become a woman-hater.

But there may be another son who is very sensitive, and suddenly he's sick at his stomach, and his emotions are hitting ten. He's getting thoughts, too: *I've got to get out of this. I just can't handle it.* And he goes to his bedroom and closes the door and cries — and then hates himself because he's too old to cry. Then thoughts come, "I'm never gonna get married. I hate this!" . . . and the seeping fog of passivity further secures its stranglehold on him.

BILL: You're right. It's pretty horrible to even think about. So what *do* I need from you when the weatherman gives his report on the radio?

ANABEL: You need me to say something like, "Now Honey, don't worry about our garden. Everyone's garden has burned to a crisp. We did what we thought was right. We prayed about it. For goodness sake, just forget it now. We'll try again next year."

BILL: Did you notice those pronouns in her statement to me? *Our . . . we . . . we'll . . .* I tell you, wife, you treat me that way, and I'll be motivated for sure! I'll pray, "Oh, thank You, Lord, for such a woman. You know how I blew that garden deal, but thank You for this dear woman who's saved my bacon in front of my sons!" And it fills me with love for Anabel, so much so, that I just want to carry her around on a silver platter — which is what every wife wants, that is, to be treasured by her husband.

If that's not your deep desire, ma'am, your feeler is stuck. I want to say something in all kindness to you, sweet sister. Your husband will never be able to carry you around on that silver platter until you choose to get on the plate and stay there.

ANABEL: We must always remember that a woman is *never* in an inferior position when she is in the place God *created* for her.

5

SEXUAL ONENESS BEYOND THE BEDROOM

*B*ILL: Let's look in on a young couple, very committed to the Lord, who are engaged to be married. Tonight, they have been to a movie. He has just kissed her good-night two or three times, and he's heading down the front walk to his car.

He's praying, "Oh Lord, I want to thank You for the grace You've showered on me by giving me the strength to keep my physical desires under control all

91

during our dating. But this is so difficult! Lord, there are still two more weeks till we get married, two more weeks to restrain myself. I know Your grace is sufficient, but if You could just let these two weeks zip by I'd certainly be grateful." He's a frustrated young man. Let's say that on a one-to-ten scale, he's fulfilled at about a four.

Now let's look in on the little bride-to-be. She's still standing with her back against the door, an enraptured look on her face. They had eaten popcorn out of the same sack at the movies, and she had slipped one of the kernels into the pocket of her sweater so she could press it in her diary. She has taken it from her pocket and is holding it close to her lips. Listen, she's praying, too: "Oh Lord, what a marvelous, glorious evening! What bliss! (She kisses the kernel of popcorn tenderly.) In two wonderful weeks we'll be married! The most glorious two weeks of my life! Lord, let me savor every wedding shower. Let me linger over every gift. Let me live each lovely experience to the fullest, so that I will be able to remember every precious moment." You can see that she is fulfilled at about an eight or maybe even a nine.†

_____

† For years I've used this illustration to demonstrate the difference between the way males and females view sex. At this point I'm not sure whether I created it or read it somewhere. If it's the latter, my apologies to its originator for not crediting it to him.

Now, when the two weeks pass, and the guy finally gets her into the castle and raises the drawbridge, his attitude is this: "All right, let's get on with this thing! Rain on that popcorn routine!" And he muffs it eighteen ways from Sunday. Guys, we have got to get it through our thick heads that we're dealing with "popcorn-type people" here.

It's not uncommon to discover in counseling sessions that if the husband feels he has an exciting sex life, he also believes he has a pretty good marriage. He might rate his marriage about a seven or an eight, and he's shocked to discover that his wife is rating it about a two because she views marriage as far more than a sexual relationship. If she is not getting her TLC needs met, her desire for sexual intimacy will be one of the first things to diminish.

It's rare to discover a case where sex is holding the marriage together. I could count on one hand the number of couples I've counseled who stated that they *both* felt they had a great sex life but that everything else was out of sync.

ANABEL: Your popcorn story illustrates *somewhat* the difference in the sexual makeup of men and women. And I say "somewhat" because the difference is so immense that it's difficult to define.

The sex act, for the woman, is the ultimate in giving and expressing love. I would have to interject here that many women today enter into this intimate relationship simply to keep from losing a particular man's companionship. But any woman would confess that it is only when the man is "her special man" that the sex act is the most fulfilling to her.

Sex, for the woman, begins at 6:00 A.M. in the way her husband says, "Good morning," and is nurtured through his tenderness, attentiveness, and kindness throughout the day. This creates the desire within her to express her love for him, and she will respond to his sexual advances. But the male can have a horrible day, no love notes or tenderness of any kind, and then see a curvy female on the way home and be ready for passionate love the moment he steps through the door. Isn't that right, Honey?

BILL: Well, how should I know? I'm a Christian, for heaven's sake! Yes, you're right on target. We don't mean to imply that sex isn't pleasurable to females, but the two genders certainly differ in their views. A survey Josh McDowell cites in one of his lectures makes the point very clear. He asked Christian singles who had engaged in premarital sex to write down the reason they had done so. The males responded, "I needed *it*;" the females stated, "I loved *him*." Consider the implications of that.

ANABEL: I doubt there is one woman reading this book who is totally free from some negative aspect of sexual intimacy. Sex has been degraded to such a level of vulgar exploitation and public display that we have to fight to keep this act holy in front of our children. It's difficult for us to remember that God created the act of sexual intercourse, that God views this act, and that it is holy before Him.

BILL: Speaking of negative aspects, an example of that would be a woman who was rejected by either her mom or dad (or both) in childhood. Remember now, a child learns about *herself* from the feedback she gets from others, and her mom is her primary female role model. If Mom sends out rejection vibes to the little girl, then she cannot relate to females. So she learns, "I'm not a feminine person. Let's face it, some are and some aren't, and I am not. Oh, how I wish I were different."

In high school she discovers that dispensing sexual favors to the boys will attract them. This "proves" to her that she *is* feminine! So she goes overboard. She will oftentimes be sexually aggressive to the point of seducing males. Do you know what I've discovered in counseling these dear, hurting women? They rarely, if ever, reach a sexual climax. Tell me, is it the sex they're after? Are they sex maniacs as Hollywood would have us believe? No. They are trying to "prove" they are feminine in order to accept themselves as female. They need this. So we're back to the same dynamic again: People need to be able to accept themselves, and they use all sorts of do-it-yourself projects in order to achieve that acceptance.

On the other hand, the woman who was rejected by her dad will often be sexually promiscuous in order to acquire male acceptance. She is willing to trade sexual favors for three hours of TLC from a male. She too, rarely, if ever, reaches a sexual climax. We can readily see that it isn't the sex she seeks, but the love, the male acceptance she's been deprived of.

Should this woman get saved, learning to rest in God's total acceptance will bring freedom from much of her intense drive for male acceptance. The first woman, in order to generate a positive, new self-image, must agree with God's Word that she has died and that she is now a new woman in Christ. This will enable her to build an entirely new, healthy, Biblical self-esteem.

ANABEL: I believe, while we're talking about negative aspects of sex, that we ought to discuss those people who have been sexually abused, both male and female. Being a victim of sexual abuse is a special problem because of the total involvement of the person. Results can range from fear to feeling "dirty"; from hate and bitterness for the person involved to hate and bitterness toward oneself; from sexual promiscuity to impotency; homosexuality to frigidity; anger to guilt, *ad infinitum* across the whole range of negative emotions.

Here's an analogy: Let's say that you are ten years old. You're out in the woods on a family outing, and you've wandered off by yourself. You hear a noise and turning, see a bear cub digging for some ants. You creep closer to watch. Suddenly, the mother bear thunders out of a thicket! She surmises you're up to no good, so she attacks. She mauls you and leaves you a mass of blood and tears. That just happens to you one time. Just once. So what is going to happen to you every time you see a bear? Even a "Gentle Ben"? Are you kidding? You *know* about bears. You've encountered one, and your emotions are "stuck" as far as bears or anything to do with bears is concerned. The minute you see a bear, you become emotionally incapacitated! Your emotional tolerance for bears is less than one point on a one-to-ten scale because your feeler is stuck on a throbbing nine!

Now, apply that story to having been sexually abused. Your emotions are stuck, and any sexual stimulus causes you such emotional discomfort that you want no part of it. You can allow this experience to keep you from ever "going into the woods" again, from ever going to the San Diego Zoo, or from even reading "The Three Bears" to your children.

BILL: Anabel and I have learned through counseling that those who have suffered sexual abuse can watch Christ overcome its effects through identifying with Him in His death, burial, and resurrection. There will still be a struggle; Satan doesn't give up that easily, but Christ through you will overcome. If the battle rages intensely, I would suggest you overtly rebuke and bind the devil and his legions for the fear they have instilled in you (stuck feeler) and offer yourself to the Holy Spirit to be filled with the peace of Jesus Christ. By properly understanding how to let Him express His

Life through you and by learning how to relax in Him, you can begin to be set free from the past no matter how intensely you have been abused. "Behold, I am the Lord, the God of all *flesh*; Is anything too difficult for Me?" (Jeremiah 32:27, emphasis added).†

ANABEL: We, as women, may use sex to control or manipulate. Too many of us have the attitude: "If you have been very good, Husband, I will reward you tonight, and we will make love. If you have not performed to suit me — meaning generally that you have not sufficiently met *my* needs — I may develop a severe headache before I go to bed, or complain about my back hurting or just how tired I am." That is not Christ living through me. You see, Christ does not cease to be my Life when I walk into my bedroom. He is my Life, period.

BILL: That's right, but because of the way our thinking has been polluted in the world, we have received the lie that we must hang the Holy Spirit on the hook in the hall as we walk through the bedroom door. It is not only appropriate, but incumbent upon me to pray, prior to entering into the sex act, "Lord, I'm trusting You to express tenderness and love through me to my wife. Use me to make this a very

---

† I highly recommend, *My Father Child* by Linda Elliott and Vicki Tanner, Ph.D. (Brentwood, TN: Wolgemuth & Hyatt, Publishers, 1988). This book, combined with the teachings of *Lifetime Guarantee*, should be very helpful.

enjoyable time for her, Lord." Great day, if we pray for mundane things like parking places, does it make sense to enter into something as significant as the sex act in our own strength?

I have counseled men who are troubled with premature ejaculation, impotency, and other sexual performance problems (not physical in origin) who have experienced significant improvement through trusting Christ as Life during the sex act with their wife. Reading the books which we suggest toward the end of this chapter is most helpful, but trusting that it is Christ's Life being expressed through you remains the key to being able to do what the books teach.

I'm certainly not teaching that Christ is having sex with my wife, for heaven's sake. *I* am the vessel; *He* is the Life of the vessel. In my shop I have an electric sander. The electricity does not sand the boards; it is simply the "life" of the sander which, in turn, enables the sander to perform as it is intended to by its creator.

ANABEL: What you said to the men about having the right mind-set is true with us too, Honey. "Lord, use me to make this all that my husband needs it to be." Setting your mind on His Life within you will give you the power you need to enter into sexual intimacy with your hubby even when that might be the last thing on earth you want to do at the time.

BILL: I recall your talking with a small group of wives one time, Anabel, where they all concurred there had been times when they had willingly responded to their husband's sexual overtures even though they themselves had not reached a climax. Their attitude during these times was one of comfort at having pleased their husband.

The message from the world via TV, movies, print, books, and magazines is that unless a husband is able to produce surefire ecstasy for his wife each time they go to bed, he's not a "real" man. That's a lie. Those scripts are written by hot-blooded individuals with vivid imaginations. Watching, listening to, or reading their lies sets people up for frustration. Let's face it, it's impossible for any human to keep on bettering his last performance indefinitely in *any* endeavor on Planet Earth. This includes the sex act.

Similarly, the world tells us that unless a wife is a tiger in bed, she is a failure as a sex partner. Another lie. The unspoken conclusion is that the husband is justified in searching for greener pastures outside his marriage vow. That, too, is a lie.

Remember, God's laws are for our supreme well-being. It isn't that by limiting us to sex with our spouse, He is a party-pooper. That's not God! I wish you could hear some of the stories I've heard from dear people who have violated this one law of God and are now struggling with the memories.

I remember a businessman who came to see me who felt that his wife was not an exciting sex partner. His secretary started inviting him over to her place, teasing him with suggestions about favors she'd do for him. He eventually fell for it, and sure enough, she was more exciting than his wife. (Bear in mind that the secretary had a hidden agenda; she wanted to take him away from his wife. So she, no doubt, was trying her best to show him what he had been "missing in life.") So then he had something to compare his wife with . . . and he'd give anything if he had never fallen in this one critical area. Sgt. Sin regularly serves up the memories to him. He would have been so much happier if he had stayed out of that greener pasture.

ANABEL: I have to somehow comprehend that my husband may come home from work and need sex because he saw a voluptuous female walking down the street, or because one of the secretaries at work dressed seductively on that particular day. (Praise God he does come home.) But, he may also have that need — intensely — because his boss chewed him out at work, or because the project that he has been researching for ten months resulted in complete failure, or because the man at the desk next to him got promoted, or because he sees me in the same dress that I have been wearing for the last year and his paycheck just won't allow me to buy a new one.

What does he need? He needs you, his wife, to assure him that he is still "the greatest," that you chose him out of all the men in the world to be just yours, and that you think he is very masculine, very strong, very capable, and you love him. He needs you to edify him.

BILL: But you know, some men have an industrial-strength sex drive. I've counseled guys who were wanting sex with their wives three times a day at age forty! Is his wife to dedicate her entire day to this guy as a sex object? Is this God's will for her? Was he just born this way? Is there no hope for her? I mean, she can't even catch the evening news living with this guy.

Invariably, I find that the Christian man with a Tarzan-size sex appetite was rejected by his folks. Here's a typical case from my files: This man was a star athlete in high school, having been named the outstanding running back in one of America's major metro centers. Guess how many games his folks attended. Zero! From that one fact you can probably guess the rest of his story. His parents never spent any time with him. He felt lonely. He felt rejected. He felt he wasn't worth their time. He felt unloved.

He got into sex his sophomore year. It was the first "love" experience he'd ever had. He promptly went overboard and began seducing every girl possible. You see, his sexual fulfillment was being *bonded* to his intensified need for love due to a lifetime of parental deprivation. He quickly learned to spell "love": s-e-x.

Ultimately, he got saved and eventually married. By forcing his wife to be the source of his love supply instead of looking to Christ as his Source, he was almost wearing the dear woman out. The guy needed love, but he didn't know of any other way to get it. He had experienced no love other than sexual love. He needed to understand his true identity in Christ, to comprehend His total love and acceptance. He needed to understand that although Christ's love is not always to be *felt*, it is always to be *believed* and, by that, *known*.

By appropriating his true identity in Christ and thus learning how to "enter into God's rest," he began to relax in his total acceptance in Christ. The Bible began to come alive to him, to reinforce this truth, and eventually his sex drive began to modify. (His wife was amazed at how the anchorman on the evening news had aged over the years.)

ANABEL: Before we leave the story of this happy couple, let me say a word to other wives who may have the same situation. Confrontation is a very necessary element in *agape* love. The verse that reads, "they [husbands] may be won without a word," (1 Peter 3:1) does not mean you never point out to your husband that he is walking "after the flesh."

I, as a wife, am aware of my husband's "flesh" problems as is no other person in his life. If I allow him to continue in this destructive unChristlike behavior, the pattern gets deeper and deeper. Who is going to confront him if I don't? Now I don't bring it up six times a day—that's nagging; rather, I broach the subject as God gives me the freedom. I pray about it, practice what I am going to say, and then, with quiet voice and apparent composure (I may be quaking on the inside with fear or anger), I point out to him his need to let Christ control him in this area. That is letting Christ *agape* him through me.

Again, we must remember that God created sex and that He intends for us to experience pleasure in that facet of His creation. He views this act. It is holy before Him. Keeping this in our minds will allow us to enter into this act of marriage with fewer inhibitions.

I admire the preacher's wife who came up to me and told me what she had given her husband for his birthday. She went to the lingerie department and chose a very risqué nightie, then to the gift wrap department and had it wrapped in masculine paper. (Raised a few eyebrows in that department.) When she presented her gift to her hubby, he said that it was one of the most appreciated gifts he had ever received. Our husbands don't want us to be the aggressors in our sexual relationships all the time, but they really love it when we occasionally surprise them. Do you agree, Husband?

BILL: Yes, that's right on. I remember counseling a couple one time, and the husband complained that his wife (a very attractive lady) wore granny gowns to bed and slept with her hair in curlers. He asked her to wear see-through nighties in the privacy of their bedroom, but she refused, stating that she saw no purpose in such a request. She said it made her feel uncomfortable to be half-dressed and that she refused to lower herself to such common behavior. Then one day I noticed her jogging through the neighborhood in flimsy nylon briefs. Apparently she wanted to look better jogging (for all the neighbor men to ogle) than she did for her husband in their own bedroom.

So to answer your original question, Hon, yes, a husband is delighted when his wife adds a spicy surprise to their sex life. I want to add, however, that sometimes a husband will make sexual demands on his wife which he might view as innovative and exciting, but which are offensive to her. If he insists that she comply with his demands, it is not Christ expressing His Life through the husband. Christ would never impose His will upon a wife just so He could get his needs satisfied. That's a flesh trip.

ANABEL: Before we close this conversation, I'd like to suggest that if your sex-life isn't all that it should be, you really might try educating yourself. You know, when you first married and found out that apple pie was your hubby's very favorite, you wanted to please him, and so you started trying recipes. He kept saying, "Nope. Not quite right yet, Sugar." (He didn't disdain eating it, however.) Finally the day came when you put a piece of pie in front of him, he tasted it and said, "This is it! Just like Momma used to make!"

Well, perfecting the sex act is much more important than baking an apple pie "just like mother used to make." There are many good books on the subject. *Love Life* and *Intended for Pleasure* by Dr. Ed Wheat, *The Act of Marriage* by Tim and Beverly LaHaye, and

Physical Unity by Shirley Rice are some we recommend.

The sex act is that *one* act that binds us together uniquely in our marriage, and it is the one way in which we are able to express our love for each other most completely.

6

TWENTY WAYS
TO LOVE YOUR WIFE

*B*ILL: Let's step into the den. I want to show you a picture on the wall and let Anabel tell you the story behind it.

ANABEL: Bill and I were presenting our seminar in a city near the ocean. It was Sunday afternoon, and you know what that means — football. Our schedule was really full, and that afternoon was going to be our only chance to explore and enjoy the beach together.

I approached the man of the house and said, "Honey, let's go for a walk on the beach."

"I'm interested in the game. Dallas is playing."

"But we won't have another chance. Our schedule is so full."

"Maybe later, but not now. Why don't you go by yourself?"

And I did. I readily confess that it wasn't at all like I had hoped it would be. It was more of a "regaining my composure" walk than that lovely stroll hand in hand down the beach that I had imagined. Sigh.

As you can see from this picture of us, though just silhouettes, strolling down the beach, he did learn from that experience.

BILL: We husbands typically do not come factory equipped to discern when our wives are saying, "Love me today by strolling down the beach hand in hand." We must *learn* these things from our wives; so Honey, why don't we pull up some chairs in front of the fireplace and have you explain to us just what a wife needs from her husband.

ANABEL: That's a good idea. I love to watch a fire, don't you?

It all begins in Genesis 3:16. I know there are a lot of different opinions about its meaning, but I like Ken Taylor's translation from *The Living Bible* which reads that a woman will desire her husband's "affections."

I was reading the *Family Weekly* periodical several years ago and came across an interview with the renowned author, Taylor Caldwell. When asked if the nine-hour TV production of her book, *Captains and Kings*, would bring her solid satisfaction, she replied:

> There is no solid satisfaction in any career for a woman like myself. There is no home, no true freedom, no hope, no joy, no expectation for tomorrow, no contentment. I would rather cook a meal for the man I love and bring him his slippers and feel myself in the protection of his arms than have all the citations and awards and honors I have received worldwide, including the Ribbon of Legion of Honor, and my properties and my bank accounts. They mean nothing to me, and I am only one among the millions of sad women like myself.

When Bill and I first began doing seminars years ago, our format was a little different. I would work with the women for a while, and he would work with the men. I would ask the women to finish a statement for me: "I wish my husband would love me by. . . ." I don't do that anymore because no matter where I went, the answers were invariably the same. However, over the years I saved all of the replies and categorized them according to the number of times each particular answer was mentioned. We want to share the "top twenty" with you.

BILL: Now, brothers, the following is what the Bible means when it says I am to love Anabel the same way Jesus loves His wife, the Church (Ephesians 5:25-27).

ANABEL: I wish my husband would love me . . .

1. By Listening to Me

This was far and away the consistent number one reply and, I might add, there are very few men who could have surmised what this first wish would be.

We were in Ennis, Texas, and I had just asked all of the women to finish the statement. I noticed one little lady who was probably in her late seventies. She began writing and when I picked the slips up, I dog-eared hers . . . I was curious. She had changed the wording a little bit, but she was asking for the same simple gift that hundreds of other women have asked for: "I wish my husband *would have loved* me by listening to me." As strange as it may seem, we never outgrow this desire. Incredible, isn't it, and so very simple.

BILL: Anabel and I have asked several groups of married couples this question: "What one thing would you say has hindered your marriage from becoming all that you dreamed it would be?" Thirty-nine out of every one hundred couples polled said that communication had been their downfall, their Waterloo.

Communication doesn't come easily. It takes a lot of time and commitment. Then, too, there are very few people who like to listen. Generally speaking, the first statement the listener hears calls to his mind a comment *he* wants to make, and that is about as far as the two-way conversation goes. Listening is a lost art.

Communication refers to the actual *practice* of discussion, which always involves at least two people. Every one of these twenty ways to love your wife in this chapter involves "communication" in one form or another. You communicate through interacting verbally, yes, but you also communicate by listening, or *not* listening; touching, or *not* touching; planning, or *not* planning; participating, or *not* participating; making eye-contact; using certain body language, certain looks, and other little acts that seem terribly insignificant to the male. As you read these twenty things, visualize what form of communication will be necessary to meet that need.

2. By Taking My "Petty Problems" Seriously

ANABEL: What do we mean by "petty problems"? Well, they can range from areas where we are insecure and need our husband to reassure us, to an area of intuitive unrest that we "just *have* to talk about, please."

Here are some examples:

"Honey, my car is making this funny noise." And generally the wife winds up feeling like an idiot because she can't explain in detail where the funny noise originates, if it has happened before, if the car is warm or cool when the noise begins, and so on and so forth.

As one woman said to me, "When I say something like that to my husband, he looks at me as though to say, 'And just what do you want *me* to do about it?'"

One of the most infamous petty problems is the grocery budget. How well I remember when we were watching our pennies, and Bill would say to me, "Honey, our money is really tight this month. Cut back on the groceries." We never cut back on anything else! Sometimes (I graciously use that word) when a wife tries to discuss the rising cost of groceries and clothes for the children, her husband communicates, in one way or another, "That's your problem. Just stay in the budget."

Here are some more "petty problems":

"The washing machine got spots of oil on the clothes when I washed today."

"I don't know whether to include the Jones in our dinner party or not."

"The toilet made a gurgling sound when I flushed it this morning."

BILL: What our gals are saying is, "I'd like for you to discuss this with me." It may be difficult for a husband to accept the importance of this problem when he's dealing with millions of dollars a day as an investor, making life and death decisions as a physician, dealing with forty-four employees as a foreman, or surviving in a job that he dislikes intensely. Maybe I've been talking to people all day and don't want to talk about any more problems. I look at my wife in disbelief, appalled that she would bother me with such mundane trivia when I have heavy things on my mind. I've got to understand that she *needs* to talk to me and needs me to show interest as I listen. Christ, through me, is able to accomplish this.

ANABEL: Listening is a common courtesy. And when I ask your advice, Husband, I am placing you in your position as my authority, as my spiritual leader. So very often, men want to be the "head of the home" because of the *power* it bestows on them. God has placed them in that role because of the *responsibility* it gives them. If you do not listen to me and give me your advice when I need it, then you do not have the prerogative of reprimanding me when I make mistakes that are wrong or even tragic. Headship involves a lot more than everyone jumping when the head says "frog."

3. By Communicating More Openly with Me

BILL: A strong, silent male can cause big problems in the marriage relationship. If he uses grunts, shrugs, eyebrows, uh-huh, huh-uh, and two-word phrases such as, "Who knows?", "Who cares?", "I'm tired.", "What's that?", and other such responses, he's not loving his wife. When the wife has this lot in life, she might start jabbering all of the time in sheer frustration, talking on the phone for hours on end, or she might just give up trying and cease all communication once the front door closes. Due to the husband's non-communicative attitude, the burden for keeping the marriage alive falls totally on the wife. Some men seem to have the idea that their only responsibility in the marriage is to bring home the paycheck, and many find out too late (after they're served with the divorce papers) that their wives could not, indeed, would not tolerate that perspective.

ANABEL: What the woman wants is someone to communicate with her on an emotional level, willing to reveal feelings, even becoming vulnerable. We call it "talking about deep things." A female is a people-centered person, an intuitive, emotional creature, and she longs to share those deep inner thoughts and feelings with her husband. In other words, she wants him to be her best friend. Difficult? Most definitely. Worth it? You bet. It is not that she wants simply to talk about herself (though that is important to her); she wants to know *your* deep feelings, your dreams, your hurts, your doubts, your secrets. That establishes a very intimate oneness, and women like that.

4. By Noticing Me More — Not Just When He Wants Sex

ANABEL: This is the only reference to sex in the top twenty. That is *not* to imply that a good sex life is unimportant to the female; but, if the only time a husband notices you is when he wants sex, then you are lowered to being a piece of equipment around the house to be used when needed. That's a pretty good definition of a mistress or a prostitute, isn't it? I'm a wife, not a mistress. I need my husband to elevate me to that position. That means including me all day long in his life as his partner. That means including me in the sex act as his *partner,* not as a sex object. P-A-R-T-N-E-R: "Someone you talk things over with; someone who engages in an activity with another; joint interests" (Webster). We can build together on that definition.

5. By Saying "Thank You" for the Little Things I Do

ANABEL: Expressing thanks has healed many a wound, encouraged many a tired soul, impressed many onlookers, and is certainly well-pleasing to God.

I'll let someone else give you her viewpoint.

I resent my husband deeply, Anabel. I resent his being gone all of the time; and if he is home, I resent him curling up with his paper on the sofa while I continue with the dishes and kids and clothes and baths and bed and on and on. I resent it that he can make it to a meeting or to work, but never to anything I would like to do. I resent his haphazard "jumping on the kids" approach to discipline. I resent having to get out of my chair to switch his TV station for him, especially when I've finally just gotten settled and he's closer to the TV anyway! And I resent my kids. I love them—OH! I do love them, but frequently I can't stand them. I guess it's that I resent being a servant to everybody and no one seems to appreciate what I do all that much. And Anabel, if I confront my husband with the way I feel, somehow it always winds up being my fault, and I wind up crying, and Anabel, I am so tired of crying.

BILL: Or from the male viewpoint:

You know, Bill, if the husband gets up every morning and goes to his eight-hour-daily and comes home to nothing but flak—someone yelling at you because you didn't do something they wanted you to do, or because you did something wrong that you tried to do; if all the kids ever do is take and take and take but never take the time to say thanks—then one day you're going to be heading for your eight-hour-daily and you're going to come to a fork in the road. One fork leads to people who see you as a money-machine, who ride you and criticize you and show no gratitude at all for what you do—the other fork leads to freedom. And you know, Bill, you're pretty tempted to take the road that leads to freedom.

ANABEL: Being grateful and expressing your gratitude to your wife works wonders:

1. It makes her feel needed.

2. It encourages her to keep going.

3. It enhances her sense of self-worth.

4. It lets others see that you are considerate of her, and she loves that.

5. It trains your children to express thanks and to appreciate her contributions to the family; for that, she especially appreciates you, Husband.

BILL: As you were saying those things, Honey, it struck me that they are just as important to the husband. That's what was missing in the life of the man who came to the fork in the road.

6. By Being Interested in My Life . . . at Least Acting Like You're Interested

BILL: Back to communication again. . . . Have you talked to people whose eyes wander as you're sharing with them? It makes you feel like they just aren't that interested. Men have to keep in mind that one of the most effective ways to communicate interest is eye-contact.

Another effective tool for showing interest is follow-up; in other words, asking questions on the subject the other party has been discussing shows that you are indeed interested in what they are saying.

Try these on your wife:

● "How did your luncheon turn out today, Honey?"

- "Hey, your hair looks nice. Do you like it?"
- "What did the doctor say about the pain in your back?"
- "How did your afternoon go at work?"

And the ultimate . . .

- "Find anything that interested you in your shopping today, Sugar? Well, try it on, and let me see how it looks."

ANABEL: Wow! Does that ever speak volumes to your wife!

BILL: And, brother, it makes no difference whether I *feel* interested or not. Jesus *is* interested, and He will express that through me if I'll *act* interested by faith. And do you know what? As you practice this, you'll eventually *become* interested.

7. By Showing Affection When Other People Are Around

ANABEL: What do you do with something that is very precious to you? Well, you look at it; you touch it; you polish it up; you check up on it regularly just to be sure all is well with it; you like to have it close to you and know exactly where it is. . . .

BILL: For instance, guys, your billfold. When I'm in a crowded area, like the airport, I'm very aware of my hip pocket. If I sense that someone is closing in on me, I take extra precautions.

ANABEL: That's what showing affection to your wife means. It gives her a sense of being protected, being secure, being precious to you. It makes her feel good because she can think, "See how nice my hubby is to me? He touches me. He likes to be close to me. He loves me."

I remember driving up to a restaurant just as another couple arrived. I don't know how old they were, but they were pretty close to being feeble. He came around — ever so slowly — and opened the door for her, then she put her arm through his, and they walked leisurely into the restaurant. And, wonder of wonders, they sat down on the same side of the booth, real close. That communicated something to me . . . tenderness, attentiveness, closeness. It was clear once again that women never outgrow these wishes.

8. By Sharing His Goals and Values with Me; Talking His Business Over with Me

ANABEL: Young mothers are the ones who feel this need most, especially after they've been carrying on not-so-stimulating conversations all day long with a two-year-old; an older woman may need it because the nest is empty, and she longs to be a part of her husband's life; all of us love it because it gives us a sense that you recognize our intelligence and that you

want us to be a part of your world. A lack of communication about your goals and work cuts me out of
the major portion of your life, Husband.

Discussing important decisions that affect the
family welfare would be included here. If you have a
chance at a job promotion, but it means moving to
Arizona — please talk to me about it. If you have the
chance to become involved in a very lucrative business endeavor, but it is just a little shady — let's talk
about it before you make me a part of something that
is against my moral values. You and I are one.

9. By Remembering Me with Little Gifts or Just Planning an Evening Out Every So Often

BILL: Two guys who are friends of ours in our
church bought weekend getaway packages (air fare
and hotel at $150.00 per couple) for themselves and
their wives as a surprise. They got sitters and enlisted
the help of a lady friend who coached them on what
clothing and make-up to pack and stow away in the
trunk of the car.

Finally, the big day arrived. They told their wives
they were taking them to dinner at a restaurant on
the far side of the Dallas-Ft. Worth Airport. As they
passed the terminal building, the driver had to turn in
to "make an important phone call." They arrived at
curbside check-in just in time to make the 6 PM flight
to Houston. Can you picture the gals' eyes as they

walked arm-in-arm with their husbands to board the plane?

ANABEL: Any wife would love that, and though hotel weekends may be out of your price range, that's all right. It isn't that I need the expensive weekend. It's the thought, the effort, and the actual *carrying out* of the plan. I know couples who have been married for years, and they still hold tenaciously to a date every week.

10. By Taking Me Out Without the Kids More — Maybe Just for a Ride

ANABEL: Women who mention this really want to pick up on "without the kids." When they go out with their husbands and take the kids with them, the stress factor increases at an exponential rate. It intensifies the pressures that she's been subjected to all day long. She takes her "office work" with her, and instead of a much-needed diversion, it can actually be an exhausting experience, a coming home to her same nightly responsibilities.

11. By Including Me in the Things He Does

ANABEL: We were talking about this with a group one time, and I had a woman say to me, "I don't need to worry about that, Anabel. My husband takes me deer hunting every season . . . to cook for him and his hunting buddies." That's not what we mean. Men may take their wives along to be a servant, a sex partner, or an audience. A wife likes to be taken as a *companion,* and her husband can make it all so very special by saying things like: "Traveling is no fun without you, Sweet. When I see interesting things I'm thinking, 'If only she were here to share this with me.' When I eat out at some fancy place, I just think how much nicer it would be to have you there with me." These comments help a wife feel included even when she can't go along very often.

12. By Trying to Understand Me

BILL: Here's that "Let's plant a big garden" concept again—*Intuition* versus *logic.* Honey, do you know what those words mean?

Logic: way of reasoning; what is expected by the working of cause and effect.

Intuition: the immediate knowing of something without the conscious use of reasoning.

ANABEL: When I tell you that I "feel" a certain way about something, my attempts at explaining *why* are usually feeble. I don't generally do that very well. Women love for men to at least *try* to "understand them," and it does take a lot of concentrated effort.

13. By Getting Involved with Things I Enjoy Doing

ANABEL: Do you remember, Husband, that as little girls we used to play dress-up, and we never could get you boys to play with us? Most women still enjoy playing dress-up, and we still have trouble getting our "boy" to play. That means going somewhere in all of my finery—with you in yours. Maybe even the ballet!

BILL: Your wife will be unique. Maybe she loves to square dance, or go for bike rides on the bike trail, or walk hand in hand on the beach, or play games with just you and another couple. Wives are admonished to "get involved," to watch the ball games with their men, go water-skiing with them, look at their guns and be impressed with their tales of conquest. Okay, it's our turn now, guys. It spices up the marriage for both of us when I get involved with some of the things my wife likes to do.

However, having a spiced-up marriage cannot be my motivation. The goal of Christ's Life is never self, but others. I am to let Him love my wife through me, meeting these very special needs that only I can satisfy.

Let me interject an admonition here. As Anabel and I discuss the needs of the wife, Sgt. Sin may be saying to the woman reader, "Oh Lord, pour it on him! I'm so glad he's hearing this." Sin will work the same number on the husband: "Lord, You sure have her where You want her now. Sock it to her!"

Listen, this book is not for your spouse to read so that you can get *your* needs met. It's for *you* to read so that you, in turn, can offer yourself to Christ in order to meet your spouse's needs. Christ lives to serve, not survive. This approach will make you a winner in His eyes.

14. By Just Holding Me in His Arms and Talking to Me

ANABEL: This letter really communicates:

When my husband came home from work yesterday, the house was a wreck and the kids were driving me wild. When I told him I just couldn't handle it, do you know what he did? He took me out into the laundry room, put his hands on my shoulders, looked down into my face and said very quietly, "Now, just calm down." Then he put his arms around me, pulled me against him and just held me for five whole minutes without saying a word. I can't explain to you how good it felt to be in his arms like that. I began to slowly relax and escape from my stressed-out world.

Then he said, "Now let's tackle this and see if we can get those little 'buzz saws' fed and into bed early tonight. Then we'll get a sitter and you and I will go to that quiet little pizza place and be together, just you and me.

Protection. Being loved. Closeness without passion. Secure. Safe from the "cold north winds" that blow about our house. Encircled in arms that are strong.

15. By Being More Tender to Me — Using Kind, Tender Words

BILL: Many men develop the "John Wayne" mindset during childhood and never stop to realize how destructive it can be. A physically big man may consider it beneath himself to be tender; a physically small man may be too threatened to be tender. A plain vanilla man may have been "trained like a bird dog" that to be tender is to be a sissy. Don't ever cry. Don't ever let your feelings show. Don't stoop to being soft.

ANABEL: But I thrive on that tenderness, dear husband. It causes me not only to respect your masculinity all the more, but to admire your sensitivity as well. Somehow, being tender with me enhances your masculinity as a whole. (See Appendix C for further teaching on what it means to be truly masculine.)

16. By Helping in the Discipline of the Children

ANABEL: I realize that being with children all day is one of my job descriptions; and I also realize that I program into our kids an awful lot of things during my nine hours with them in contrast to your three or four hours with them in the evenings, Daddy. I would like for you to realize that.

BILL: Brother, what if you worked under one boss from 7:30 A.M. until 6:30 P.M. and then had another person come in and set up entirely different standards and procedures? That would cause no small amount of frustration and confusion, wouldn't it? That's how my wife and kids feel if I come home each evening with a different way of doing things.

ANABEL: We simply need to work together and be consistent in what we do with the children. I don't want to cut you out of their lives through the day, and I refuse to use you as the "big, bad bear" who is going to appear around dark and "then you kids will be sorry!" I want to let my children see that I respect you, that I am under your authority, that I don't wear the pants in the family, and that you and I agree about certain areas in our lives, especially where they are concerned. I have security when the children understand that if they sass me, they answer to you. How I admired the man who said to his rebellious teen-age son, "You're not going to treat *my wife* that way." A wife really knows whose side her husband is on if he says something like that.

But, it falls pretty flat if you don't catch the ball when I throw it to you. Here's a pass that was fumbled:

Wife: "Something is bothering Junior."

Husband: "How do you know that?"

Wife: "He's throwing his toys, trying to kick Cissy. I can just tell that he's upset about something."

Husband: "Oh, you're always getting these notions. Just forget it."

Wife: "But, dear, he needs our help."

Husband: "He'll grow out of it."

Of course, parents accomplish "oneness" in the area of discipline through that magic word again, "communication" — talking through things after the kids are in bed, perhaps disagreeing at times, but knowing that we will present a united front in the morning and that when you come home, there will obviously be two of us agreeing . . . "working together." A wife really does need that.

17. By Saying Little Things — Words of Caring, Compliments, Appreciation

ANABEL: By noticing and saying the little things, you will be telling me that you love me (caring), that you think I am really pretty great, that you want to convey to me that you appreciate me for who I am (compliments), and that you also acknowledge positively what I do (appreciation). All of these will build my sense of self-worth.

BILL: Of course, we each have to have our sense of self-worth focused on who we are now that we are in Christ Jesus, but it surely makes life a lot nicer if my spouse will help me with my earthly needs and encourage me.

18. By Accepting Me Just As I Am

ANABEL: This covers my physical appearance, my performance, my achievements, my character, my mannerisms . . . all of the things that make me who I am.

I remember meeting a woman for lunch one day to talk with her. We both ordered French onion soup, but when she began telling me about what was happening in her marriage, neither of us touched our soup.

For instance, she said that her husband would pick out some woman and comment several times about her, "I really like the way she wears her hair. Why don't you fix yours that way, Nancy?" So she would find out where the woman had her hair done, go to the shop, and say, "Fix it like hers." Yet her husband would never notice. He would do the same thing with clothes, even shoes. He never overtly said to her, "You don't measure up to the women I admire," but it was communicated to her very painfully by inference.

BILL: Remember, too, that you must *earn* the right to point out a person's mistakes and faults by demonstrating a life-style of consistent encouragement. You earn that right with your wife by "saying words of caring, giving compliments, and expressing appreciation." When you do this, she will be able to hear you when you center on something you believe she needs to change.

19. Spending More Time with the Family

BILL: It may seem that we're contradicting ourselves when we say on the one hand, "take your wife out without the kids more often," and on the other, "spend more time with the family." We're not. She needs the time away, yes, but it thrills her when you plan family outings, when you agree to take little Clair for her dancing lessons or manage to be there for Junior's soccer game, when you take your son fishing or your daughter out for breakfast.

I've counseled enough to know what happens with an absentee father. I don't want that, and I know that you don't want that either. You love your children just as I do. Remember the old saying, "An ounce of prevention is worth a pound of cure"? What a tragedy it would be to have to look back one day and say, "If only. . . ."

20. By Making Me Feel Like a Woman

ANABEL: When Adam said, "This is now bone of my bones, and flesh of my flesh; She shall be called Woman . . ." (Genesis 2:23), I imagine that Eve *felt* like something very special — a woman, not just another animal in the garden menagerie. And I imagine that she could catch Adam looking at her throughout the day and experience that same feeling.

I suppose "desirable" would be a word to describe what I'm trying to say; it means, "worth having; pleasing." Opening car doors, helping me with my chair, offering assistance when I'm undertaking something that is hard for me to do — these simple, little things give me that feeling of being "special" to you.

A male still likes to feel masculine even when he is eighty years old. We women are no different. My need to feel feminine does not somehow disappear or diminish when I'm married, when the kids are grown and gone, or when I'm eighty years old. No, I'll need it until the day I die. (See Appendix B for further teaching on femininity.)

Now, Honey, before we close I want to say just a word to a very special group.

An angry young woman approached me one night after we had been discussing the needs of the woman in a seminar. Essentially, this was what she said, "My husband is my husband in name only, Anabel. I've been getting along as well as could be expected, but you have torn open my heart and uncovered all of these desires. I never knew what was causing my un-happiness and the turbulence in my soul. Now you have made me aware of these needs, and my emotions are screaming at me for tenderness and companion-ship and all of the things that I will never have! I would have been better off if I had never known!"

Many of you women who are reading this live as she lives . . . single women, widows, the single-again woman, that woman whose husband is not truly loving her at all. What are you to do? Are you to suffer through life without having this need for tenderness met? Without a companion? Without being loved? Cherished? Respected? Can these deep needs be met only by a physical husband, an earthly mate?

Oh, my dear ones, is Christ limited and unable to satisfy this need for you? "Behold, I am the Lord, the God of all flesh; is anything too difficult for Me?" (Jeremiah 32:27). He is able. You are His beloved bride and He longs to meet your every need. I can walk with the poise and confidence of a woman who knows she is loved and cherished. I can accept all the exquisite gifts that my husband so lovingly sends to me (be they wild flowers, clouds, trees, or birds . . .). I can walk with Him and I can talk with Him and I can hear Him say, "You are mine and I love you deeply." How I cherish the thought of every person who walks alone, unloved in this world, grasping and clinging tenaciously to the indescribable, unsurpassed, constant, and tender love of the Bridegroom, Jesus Christ.†

---

† *Faithful . . . Forever*, Anabel Gillham, Gillham Ministries, Ft. Worth, Tx.

7

HOW WIVES
SPELL LOVE

A NABEL: This letter came from a precious young wife who was drowning while crying out to her husband, "Love me."

Dear Anabel,

I can only begin this letter by saying that if the pain that we are all now suffering were physical, I'm sure the wound would be fatal. It never ceases to amaze me how much emotional trauma one can withstand.

Our last counselor told Mike that as long as he had someone to lean on, he would. Hopefully, on his own he will find the self-motivation he needs. I love my husband very much and am as concerned for his well-being as I am for my own and the children's, but I'm just so weary. My self-survival alarm is buzzing and manifesting itself in weight loss, amnesia, and sleeplessness.

I feel guilty and somewhat selfish to be the one to say, "I quit," but I am scared and don't really know what else to do. If only this could be what Mike needs. I know the conflict between our needs and the fact that neither of us is able to satisfy those needs is destroying both of us, regardless of how much we still love each other. It is as though we are groping and drowning in our pain, fear, and frustration, reaching out to each other for help, but our arms just aren't long enough to bridge the gap. And if you tread water long enough, the fear of sinking eventually changes to a blessed relief and you no longer fear it, but welcome it.

I have shortchanged Mike in many ways, too. It's a vicious circle. Mike doesn't satisfy my needs as a husband or father on a daily "let's function together and get it done" basis. I don't like it when I carry all the responsibilities, so I build resentment toward him. This reduces my ability to give and show him the affection and praise *he* so desperately needs. Therefore he escapes and seeks it elsewhere, leaving me back where we started, doing it alone. It's an 'I will if you will' situation, but it has reached the point where neither of us *can* let alone *will*.

At first I had such horrible doubts: What about the kids, what about money, will Mike be all right, can he get up with an alarm, can he find his own socks, and for heaven's sake, can I withstand the pain when the kids ask why Daddy lives somewhere else?

Through the bedroom window I can see the plum tree full of green leaves. A month ago it was just a stump with dry, bare branches, but spring came just like it always does. I'm sure that spring will come again for us and that after this winter is over we can be fruitful again. We just need some time to trim and prune. We already have two blossoms that need us both, but not as we are now. I'll close with this thought: "Please Lord, teach us to laugh again. But God, don't ever let us forget that we cried."

That poor husband didn't know *how* his wife spelled love; and even if he *had* known, he didn't know *where* to get the power to meet her needs. Honey, there must be millions of marriages with problems similar to this one.

BILL: Ephesians 5:25-27 reads,

Husbands, love your wives, just as Christ also loved the church and gave Himself up for her; that He might sanctify her, having cleansed her by the washing of water with the word, that He might present to Himself the church in all her glory, having no spot or wrinkle or any such thing; but that she should be holy and blameless.

That's the way I'm commanded to love you, Sugar. This means far more than having warm, fuzzy feelings toward you, doesn't it? All those hundreds of women whose responses you compiled in the last chapter were, in effect, telling us husbands how women spell love, right? Look at the pronouns in the passage above. The church is referred to as "her." We husbands are to take our cue on how to love our wives from Jesus' relationship to *His* wife.

ANABEL: You're absolutely right. There is one other thing that I want to point out before we move on. Did you discover in the verse above just what it was Jesus gave His wife as an expression of His love?

BILL: Yes, He gave "Himself."

ANABEL: That's what you are to give to me, Husband. Oh, you can go along with all of the suggestions that we've already given and master the ones we're about to elaborate on, but none of it will be satisfying to me nor fulfilling to you if you do not first give me *yourself*. Otherwise, these truths will come through to both of us as laws that you feel obligated to keep; and I'll feel that you're trying to either appease or manipu-

late me. All of the actions mean nothing without relationship.

I remember one woman who sat in my office with
diamonds in her ears, on her fingers, and around her
neck. Her beautiful mink coat was thrown over the
back of the chair. Her face was buried in her arms and
her body was shaking with sobs. Finally, she raised her
head, lifted her chin defiantly, and said with great disdain, "Look at me, Anabel. I'm loved."

I have often said that I would rather be under the
directive of Ephesians 5:22 than with you, Husband,
under that of Ephesians 5:25. You very obviously have
the more difficult responsibility. It's just that someone
saw the "Wives, SUBMIT!" and incorporated that
Biblical gem into our marriages; yours says, "Husband,
DIE!"

BILL: The word *love* in verse 25 is *agape* in the
Greek, meaning "I will *do* the most constructive,
edifying, redemptive thing I can for you." That's *performance*, not feeling. And notice the phrase, "gave
Himself up." How many rights does a man have who
gives himself up for someone? None. Now I can't do
that, but Christ can through me.

It would be possible for me to admire you, feel
deep romantic attachment to you, etc., and yet be ig-
norant of just how to *agape* you as Christ *agapes* His
wife, wouldn't it, Hon? First of all, I must learn *how* to
love you by listening to you. Small wonder that the

need for husbands to listen is what the majority of the wives listed as their number one desire!

ANABEL: Bill and I searched the scriptures and discovered six ways that we believe Christ loves His wife. As Bill previously mentioned, if Christ does these things for His "wife" and my husband is to "love me as Christ loves His wife (the Church)," then these things are given to instruct my husband in just what it is that I need.

1. Jesus Longs for Her to Know
Just How Much He Loves Her

BILL: How can I emulate Christ's love to let my wife know just how much I love her? Well, how about simply *telling* her, "I love you"? I've counseled men who couldn't say this to their wives. I remember one man who had told his wife ten years ago that if he ever stopped loving her he'd let her know. Bless his heart, that's as tender and loving a message as he could muster up in order to express love to his wife.

ANABEL: I talked to his wife. Her perception was so much different. She looked at me with tears in her eyes and said, "Anabel, my husband hasn't told me that he loves me in ten years!"

BILL: Why would this be hard for him to do? He would probably say that it just runs in his family, that none of his clan ever said "I love you" to each other or to their wives or to their children, and that he's just like his father and his brothers. He views it as genetic! It's not genetic—his feeler is stuck! Consequently, he considers himself unlovable, unworthy of receiving love, and unable to express it to others. He can't give what he doesn't have.

His emotions stayed lined up on that perception for so long that they eventually became stuck, and now he *feels* inhibited about verbalizing love at level eight even on his best days! If he were to try to say, "I love you," he'd *feel* like the sky was caving in on his head. He can't do it, but Christ *through* him is able.

I recall another man, a dedicated Christian, who had not told his wife he loved her in over twenty years. He, like the man above, had been rejected in childhood. At about age eleven he was walking home from school with a "worldly woman" of twelve who suggested it might be fun to kiss each other. He agreed and gave her a peck on the cheek. She said, "No! This is the way you kiss!" She then kissed him square on the mouth till the bells went off. He'd never felt anything so zingy in all his born days! (Do you remember your first special kiss?)

Though he searched the whole world over to find a female who could consistently make the "bells of St. Mary's" go off when he kissed her, he never did. He eventually got married, even though he *felt* like he had missed the "right" woman. Consequently, he didn't *feel* as though he *really* loved his wife and could never tell her that he did. That would make him a phony, and he couldn't handle that; so, his wife lived with him for over twenty years but never heard those words she longed with all her heart to hear.

God didn't command me to express my love to Anabel when I *felt* like it. He said simply that I was to *do* it. "But Bill, if I were to tell my wife that I love her when in fact I don't *feel* love for her, that would make me a hypocrite, would it not?" Well, let's examine the definition of the word *hypocrite* and find out.

H-Y-P-O-C-R-I-T-E: "Pretending to be what one is not" (Webster). Most folks have swallowed Satan's definition: "Acting contrary to how you *feel*." That's a lie! As one would suspect, the world subscribes to Satan's definition, and alas, most Christians, even many Christian counselors, apparently do as well. They focus their emphasis on what your feeler "says." Counselors tell us to "get in touch with our feelings" as though they were our *primary barometer of truth*; we are told that expressing our true feelings is being honest, and that if we don't have the feelings we once had for our spouse, it is dishonest to stay in the marriage. They'd have us be controlled by our fickle feelers!

Brother, Christ is your Life (see Colossians 3:4a). If you were, by faith, to haul off and claim that Christ is expressing His Life through you, and then say to your wife, "I love you, Susie," would you be pretending to be what you are not, or would you indeed be acting like what you *are*? Do you see it? You would be acting like something is true which *is* true! You'd be "walking in the light" instead of being controlled by your emotions.

Let me walk you through a little exercise to help you appropriate Jesus as your Life and overcome this stuck feeler.

> *Step One:* You can know all there is to know about how to operate your computer, and you can type till your heart's content, but if you never turn it on, your typing will be powerless. *Claim your power—* Christ as Life by faith. You use the same faith you used to get saved. You claimed Him as Savior and Lord, and now you're claiming Him as *Life*. This "turns the switch on." You pray, "Jesus, I surrender all that I am to You so that You, in turn, may express Your Life through me. I mean this with every fiber of my being. I give up. No strings, no deals, no hidden agenda on my part. You take over and live through me."

> *Step Two:* Get up off your knees believing Jesus is *now* expressing His Life through you and begin to *act* like it's true. This is where the power lies in living the Christian life. If you try to wait until you *feel* Him start living through you, you'll never get off dead center. It's done by faith and obedience, not by feel.

I have found that to jump right in and say, "I love you, Susie," is a tough assignment for a man whose feeler is stuck on nine, but we can make it easier. If you're one of these guys, stretch your emotions slowly. Set your wrist alarm for 2:00 A.M., lie there in the dark staring at the ceiling, and say, "Okay, Lord, here goes. You're going to do this through me. Ready?" And you whisper, "I love you, Susie." And she's still sawing logs! That's okay! I'm serious. You have started the ball rolling, and Christ did it for you, through you! Just keep doing it.

Next time write it to her, then tell her over the phone, then holler it from the car as you drive away. You'll finally get to where you can actually look her in the eyes and tell her. Aw, come on, brother, do it. Satan is keeping you from loving your wife through your stuck feeler. You don't want to let him keep on doing that to you. Fight like the new man you are in Christ.

Keep working at tenderness and believe, by faith, that Jesus is tearing down those strongholds which *you* have developed and strengthened over the years by playing "lord of the ring." He'll do it, man. It may not happen in a big flash of light, and that's all right. No man totally overcomes the flesh on this planet. But as you practice this process and time progresses, you'll get more and more freedom from those lifelong hangups. You'll love the results and so will your wife.

And if I don't do this? What if I continue to let Sgt. Sin control me through my feelings and clam up? *Now* I am "pretending to be what I am *not*." That makes me a phony by God's definition. A hypocrite. I am acting differently from who God says I am in Christ.

ANABEL: I have had women tell me something to this effect: "Anabel, I don't want to be critical of my husband. He's a good man and has always provided well for his family. But I so yearn for gentleness, for tenderness, for him to touch me and tell me that he loves me.

"You will probably laugh at me or think I am terrible, but my teen-age daughter has created such a discontent in my relationship with my husband. I actually envy her at times. I'm not too old to dress up and go out on the town. Oh, how I would love it! I guess he thinks that going camping should suffice. I know — I'm awful. He's a good husband, Anabel, and I should be thankful for him just the way he is."

BILL: You know, Hon, sometimes we males don't *hear* very well. You might be telling me that you want to "put on the dog" and go do the town at level ten, but I hear you telling me at level two. I have found it very helpful for you to put a number on your requests; for instance, when you say, "Honey, I'd like for you to get the battery in my car fixed and that's a nine," it communicates to me that I should jump on it and get it done.

Once I began to allow Christ to use me to express *verbal* love to Anabel, He began to reveal new and creative ways to say, "I love you." I don't mean in

French or some new language, but in *actions!* Actions do speak louder than words.

I recall a time when it was our William's birthday. We make a big deal of birthdays in our home by loading the birthday person down with gifts. We also limit family giving at Christmas in order to load Jesus down on *His* birthday.

At any rate, Will had expressed a desire for a certain gift. Anabel wanted to get it, but I didn't think we should and subsequently made the decision not to do so. Later, I began to feel she was right, so I went down and purchased it without telling her.

On birthday morning, I slipped the secret package into the pile and then sat back to watch both Will's and Anabel's reactions. As he picked it up, her brow furrowed in curiosity because she didn't recognize the package. I was looking like the cat that had swallowed the mouse.

Anabel was shocked when he opened the gift. She quickly looked at me, smiled, and her eyes began to brim up a little. It was then that the Holy Spirit let me know that I had just said to her, "I love you, Anabel." I didn't know . . . I hadn't known that this was a way to tell my wife that I loved her.

Hon, it seems that moms have a different relationship with their kids than we dads. You'd rather I buy a watch for one of our sons or spend time working with him on his car than to do the same for you, wouldn't you?

ANABEL: Yes. Even though I love for you to do kind things for me and give me things, it expresses a special sort of love message to me when you are kind to our sons.

BILL: Brother, there must be dozens of ways to "say" to our wives, "I love you," but unless I hold a good funeral for my old ways and allow Jesus to begin to live His Life through me, I may never discover them.

2. She Is His Consuming Desire

ANABEL: Let's place this second way Christ loves His Bride on an attainable level for you, Husband. Would you simply *think* of me often and let me know someway that you are thinking about me?

Bill has done such a beautiful job of this and, at the same time, has trained the boys, so I am very blessed. It all began when they were little, and they'd go out to the woods with their dad. Invariably, one of them would bring me a rock from their trip. I don't mean a polished rock; I mean a creek pebble. Now, just what did that little pebble communicate to me? "Here's something for you, Mom, to let you know that I was thinking about you while we were gone."

One of the most delightful things Bill ever did to show me he was thinking of me was when he came home one day from a trip and said, "I brought you something." That was almost to be expected because he was so good that way, but the "something" was generally in a corner of the suitcase wrapped in his dirty clothes. Not so this time. It was a big box — probably two feet square. I couldn't imagine! You know what it was? A *huge* pumpkin! I loved it!

Now you may be thinking, "So what was he saying . . . make some pumpkin pies?" Wrong. Listen carefully. My men rarely bring me remembrances from the jewelry store or the department store. You see, they have *listened* to me over the years — they know me — and they know what I like. I have some very delicate little feathers tucked in my Bible and a sprig of greenery from a redwood tree in Yosemite; I have some black bean pods on the buffet and some stuffed animals that have come to live with us. All of these things say, "You were on my mind."

Bill not only remembers special days; he does what we mentioned in the very beginning: He makes some very difficult days special by letting me know in some way that he is thinking about me.

BILL: You mean like calling you from the office mid-morning just to see how you're doing. . . . However, calling to see if you remembered to pick up the cleaning doesn't count, does it?

ANABEL: Well, you might have to *start* with something like that.

BILL: Right. But it *should* be simply to say I love you or that I am praying for you when I know your day is very busy and that you are, perhaps, struggling.

Or I could call and say, "Honey, how about picking me up for lunch and we'll go get a Whataburger?" Or if we're in a motel while doing a seminar and on my morning run I pick a little wild flower and put it in a glass by the lavatory so it will greet you when you turn on the light . . . you like things like that, don't you?

ANABEL: Yes, they tell me that you're thinking about me when we're apart and that I occupy a very important place in your life. And little gifts like the wildflower are evidence to me that you know me . . . that you really listen to me.

BILL: Honey, put a number on how important that is to you. How much do things like that mean to you?

ANABEL: Oh, it's a ten. All of these things are tens to me. This is how my husband is to love me. God created me with these needs, and He desires that my husband meet them by offering himself up to Christ.

8

HAVE YOU NOTICED YOUR WIFE LATELY?

A NABEL: Every word, every action is important. Look at the ways Christ loves His Bride that we discussed in the previous chapter; once again it would seem that we are looking at the impossible.

3. Every Word, Every Action Brings Honor and Expresses His Devotion to Her.

Honey, I think we need to go back to the very beginning and consider once more that plaintive, "listen to me." Listening expresses honor and devotion, but let's add to that, "sharing your life with me." That gives you an obtainable goal, doesn't it? *Listen to me* and *share your life* with me.

Dear Anabel,

I guess I just need someone to help me understand what's going on. Let me try to explain.

It's my job to take care of the washing at home, and I'm not complaining about that. But my washing machine broke. I told my husband about it and he suggested that I go to the neighborhood laundry for a while because he didn't "have the time to look into it just now." A couple of weeks later, I mentioned it to him again and he, rather gruffly, agreed to check it out. He's really handy with things like that. It needed a new part, so he called and ordered one from Sears. It arrived a week later, but it was the wrong part. He finally got around to ordering the replacement. It came about a week ago and is still in the box in the garage.

Now here is my dilemma.

My husband came home from work and told me how his secretary's computer had gone on the blink at 10:00 that morning and how he had called the office machines' repair shop and told them to get over there on the double—"We have some important mail to get out." They didn't come, so he called back and told them that if they weren't coming to repair it they should bring him a replacement. "We can't get our work done around here without it."

He is not in love with his secretary. She's a super secretary, he tells me that regularly, but that is not the issue. What bothers me is that her work is so important and mine is *not*. When the "tools" I need to get my work done break, he doesn't set any records repairing them.

The only way I can put all this together is that what I do must not be very important to my husband. He doesn't seem to notice, and he doesn't listen when I talk to him about it or fix "my tools" when I tell him that they're broken.

BILL: How can I prove to you that I am listening, Hon? This is something I have had to work at, and, though I haven't *arrived* as yet, it's exciting to me that the Lord has granted me some growth in this area.

I can *make eye contact.* I can *give my undivided attention* to you. This means getting away from the ball game on TV or laying my paper down while we talk. Even though I may truly be listening as I watch the news, I have learned that when it is important to *prove* to Anabel that I am listening, I need to turn the sound off and turn my back to it or walk out of the room with her. As I trust Christ to live His Life through me, the Holy Spirit will make me sensitive to when this is necessary. I must refuse to see this as "silly" and realize it is all a part of loving her. It's very important that I change my views to conform to those of Christ's.

Another thing I can do, Hon, is *take some action on whatever concern of yours you discuss with me.* For instance, our lawn is sodded with St. Augustine grass and heavily shaded. I have learned by listening that you like a pretty lawn. One of the ways I "love you" is by working on it. You have mentioned on a couple of occasions that you're concerned because a large area under one of the trees is getting barren looking, and you've wondered aloud if we don't need to do something about it.

You overhear me making phone calls to nurseries that handle grass sod, checking on prices, which strain of grass they recommend, how much to water it in order to ensure that it will live, etc. Then you hear me announce that I am going to resod the bare spot under the tree. The following Saturday I conscript a couple of helpers (sons) as the day approaches, hook up the trailer, drive off with my two helpers staring glassy-eyed into the sunrise, return with a load of grass sod, and cover the big bare spot. What does this "say" to you?

ANABEL: You've no idea how many things that says to me. The main one is, of course, that you actually listened to me. Then, you considered what I said as important. Finally, you gave it some thought, and now you're going to take action. There is such a deep emotion that wells up within a woman when she sees her husband walking through the house with his screwdriver in his hand. He's fixing the nest! And that's what your visit to the nursery says to me: "He's fixing the nest." How many women have said to me in different ways, "If only my husband would take some interest in our home." It builds a oneness. It fosters security.

BILL: Or how about when you share with me a concern you have about one of the boys? You don't get good vibes from a new friend he's hanging around with, and you want me to talk to him about it. I give it some thought while I sit on it a couple of days. Then I come back to you and reopen the conversation by saying, "You know when you mentioned your apprehension over Wade's friend the other day? I've been thinking and praying about it, and I have an idea." Then I proceed to share my idea with you. You may or may not agree that my idea is a good one, but what would this episode "say" to you?

ANABEL: As you've already mentioned, Honey, there is a different bond between a mother and her children than there is between the dad and his child.

Solomon stripped bare a mother's heart when he suggested cutting the baby in half to settle an argument. God says, "Can a woman forget her nursing child, and have no compassion on the son of her womb? Even these may forget, but I will not forget you" (Isaiah 49:15). He's saying that it is incredulous that a woman would forget her child. There's a special attachment. And when you, as my husband, sense that fusion and let me express my thoughts to you about one of our kids, it meets a deep, deep need in my life. How many times I have said, "Honey, could I talk to you about the boys for just a few minutes?" What I'm saying is, "I sense a problem, and I want you to be involved and help me." I may not be correct in my assessment, but I want you to take me seriously. It's important to me.

BILL: You know, we males can get every one of our basic needs met (with the exception of sex) right out there in the world and still pass as "godly men" in most churches. We can get our need for authority, praise, significance, or achievement satisfied from the world, and most folks will never know how we are depriving our wives of the love God has commanded that we give them.

I can be a physician and have the mothers in town referring to me as "dear old Dr. Bill." That feels great! Or I can run the motor pool at the office and have the sales force bowing to my authority, even those who make twice the salary I make. The flesh grooves on that! I can be a cop and experience the important man in the Lincoln calling me "Sir" as I write him up. The flesh loves it! All of these things can satisfy the masculine needs I have, and if I play the game this way, the flesh, being fickle, requires that each new year (or even week) *must* bring me greater and greater satisfaction from the world. This is one of the major catalysts that produce the mid-life crisis in some men. They're searching for the ultimate flesh trip, and tragically, many believers are searching through psychotherapy for *its* answer to the problem. The answer is that the man must come to the end of himself and his fleshly techniques for getting his needs met.

Whereas I, as a male, am able to meet my needs carnally via the world system, Anabel (as female) cannot optimally satisfy her feminine needs through gaining ever-increasing authority in the world. God has so designed the female that her needs are to be satisfied through her husband, the main man in her life. The typical new woman in Christ isn't tempted by the authority game as we males are. My wife needs me to love her as Christ loves His wife, and if I don't do that, I am sinning against her and against God.

ANABEL: I remember a couple we were talking with in their luxurious home. The husband was venting his wrath, and at the height of his tirade he flung his arm out in the direction of the lavish rooms and said, "Look at everything I have given you! You don't want for a thing! And all I ask from you is sex, and you won't give it to me!

She looked at him with tears running down her cheeks and said, "Is that *all* you need me for? I would gladly give up all of this just to have you."

That man was getting all of *his* needs met out in the world system, except his need for physical fulfillment. He couldn't understand why his wife resisted his advances and began to withdraw from him. Begin to take notice in your world . . . a woman may leave money and social prestige for a man who can offer her nothing but a very small house with a chain link fence. Why? Because he loves *her.*

BILL: Admittedly, some Christian women are into the authority game, but I have discovered these women were reared in an environment where pressure for high achievement was either applied by their folks or they applied it to themselves. It was the key to getting love in their childhood environment, whether spoken or implied, and they are still striving to satisfy their need for *self*-acceptance through achievement. That's their flesh, not their spirit.

I don't mean to be critical of any brother, but there is a unique occupation which affords the male a golden opportunity to feed his need for authority and female praise, and that is the pastorate. How many men, with hearts seeking to please the Lord, put in a seventy-to-ninety hour workweek at the church only to come home at 9:00 P.M. too tired even to toss his faithful wife a few TLC crumbs? He's poured out all the TLC supply he had on the church. I believe Jesus is saying to this well-meaning brother, "You are spending too much time with My wife. I instructed you to pour your life into *your* wife as well as Mine (see

Ephesians 5:25-27), but you're spending so much time with Mine that you have no time for your own."

Many wives of church staffers are starving for the love that God has commanded their husbands to give them, but the husbands are too busy giving it to the "redhead" (their work). A man must come to the end of himself on this if he is to go on with God. Let's face it, male flesh finds it stimulating and fulfilling to get its needs for authority and praise satisfied from a smorgasbord of women in the church rather than from only one; and tragically, the flesh being what it is, this scene can evolve into a sexual one in literally "the twinkling of an eye."

ANABEL: I've heard you call this "emotional adultery," Honey. That means giving of yourself emotionally to others all day long to the extent that when you get home, you're too emotionally drained to listen to your wife's problems or be sensitive to *her* needs. This would be doubly difficult for me if the people you were giving your emotions to were women. Let's think this through. Someone is going to have to suffer, either your counselees, your staff, the secretary who may be sharing her marital problems with you through many tears . . . or your wife. Who is *your* God-given responsibility? You are setting your wife up for the mailman who comes by and says, "It's always nice to get to your house, Mrs. Jones. You make my day with your friendliness."

BILL: God's Word to the first husband on Planet Earth was that his wife was to be his number one responsibility among humans, and that he was even to "leave his father and his mother, and cleave to his wife" (see Genesis 2:24) in order to accomplish this. He said this before there were even fathers and mothers, and it hasn't changed. I am to seek Jesus first (see Philippians 3:10), but Anabel, not my work nor my ministry, comes second. Everyone else follows Anabel.

I have counseled many folks who were rejected by a dad who *naively* poured his life into his work and neglected his family.

I think of the woman who came to see me. All her formative years she had sought her busy-in-the-church dad's attention. She even gave up high school ball games in order to study and attain the good grades she hoped would please him. She was named valedictorian! She practiced diligently for her address at the graduation exercises. "Dad's going to be there. He'll be so proud of me." He missed it to drive the bus for the senior-adults spring foliage tour. "I can't come, Honey. They're depending on me to be there." I ask you, was he being led by the Holy Spirit or by his flesh?

I think of a layman, a man of God. For years he wouldn't come home after work until he had won at least one soul to Christ. Many people were won to Christ, that is many except in his own house. I love this man and his family, but he was wrong. He made a tragic mistake. My dear brother, that price is too high to pay.

4. He Lives That She Might Come into Existence and Be Set Apart

ANABEL: Once again, Bill, let's put this on the practical level. How about just *being aware of me and my needs?*

As you have already come to see through our testimonies, Bill and I were *not* meeting each other's needs in the early years of our marriage.

This story begins very innocently at church. Our young married couples met together on Sunday evening, and on this particular Sunday night, I had been asked to present a small part on the program. When I finished, I went back and sat down by a young man whom I'll call Don. Don leaned over and whispered to me, "You enjoy doing things like that, don't you?" I looked at him and said, "Why, yes. How did you know that?" (That's the performer in me, remember?) Then he said words that every woman loves to hear from a man: "Oh, I think I understand you." A man who understood me or was even interested in trying to understand me . . . I liked that.

So with that small exchange, I began the womanly process of manipulation. When we would gather for church after our meeting, I would always arrange it so we would sit by Don and his wife. He didn't mind. We were playing a game.

I began evaluating his relationship with his wife. If she were talking to me and Don entered into the conversation, her whole countenance would change, and she would be gruff and hateful with him. I never shall forget the night we were having a spaghetti supper at our house. I was standing by the stove, stirring the meat sauce. She was standing there talking with me. Don came up and slipped his arms around her waist. She flung them off and said, "Get away from me! You bother me!" You can easily see that Don was not getting his needs met, I was not getting my needs met, and we were embarking on an exciting new adventure together.

Don was very *aware* of me. I made all of my own clothes. I could work on a dress for weeks and even have Bill check the hemline, but still he would not notice enough to say anything nice about it *or* me. But, I could always count on Don.

BILL: Good ol' Don. You could always count on good ol' Don.

ANABEL: He would see me at church and say, "Hey, you have on a new dress. It's very becoming." I needed that, but it all came to a screeching halt one Sunday evening. Don and I were walking by ourselves over to the church building. (Bill didn't care where I walked or who I walked with. He was with a group of people telling his "funnies," and they were laughing at him. I didn't laugh at Bill. Nothing he did was funny. Bill hurt.) Don said to me with a very intimate tone in his voice, "You look so pretty tonight, Anabel." Women can recognize an intimate overture, and I didn't want that. All I wanted was his attention. So, in an effort to lighten a heavy scene I said, "Oh, Don, you just see me on Sunday when I've really tried to look my best. You should see me some Monday." He said, "I'd like to. May I?" The game was over for me. I didn't want intimacy, so I didn't let it go any further. But Don found another woman who was hurting as badly as he was hurting, and two marriages ended in tragic divorces.

Husband, I really do want to wear my hair the way you like it, but how am I ever going to know unless you say to me, "I love your hair that way." Husband, I *want* to dress for you, to please you, but I won't know what you want if you never notice me and say, "That's my favorite color on you." I need that!

BILL: Sgt. Sin may be "saying" to you, "Well, I'm just not that way. I don't care how she wears her hair or what she wears. I don't notice things like that. My dad was that way and so am I. I can't help it; you can't change the spots on a leopard. She's going to have to realize this and accept me as I am."

That's all flesh, my brother. That old man died, and you are a brand new model. Jesus is now your Life. Will *He* be able to make comments about your wife's hair through you if you'll move your lips and believe He is doing it? Of course. But, you must come to the end of yourself and your fleshly ways if it's ever going to happen. Do it, brother. Three years from now you won't believe the changes that will have taken place in you.

Anabel: I remember a phone call that came early one morning from a woman who related a story that I've heard time and time again. She said, "Anabel, a 'Don' came into my life, but I didn't get out when he asked for intimacy. Now I'm in an affair and it has destroyed my family. Oh Anabel, what can I do? I never intended for it to escalate to this point, but I so needed the man's tenderness and attention. . . ."

How long has it been since you have said to your wife, "You look so pretty tonight, Sweetheart"? How long since you've noticed her hair on the day when she comes home from the beauty shop? How long since you have told her just how much you appreciate all of the little things that she does to make herself attractive for just you? I need you to *be aware of me*, Husband.

9

RED PENCILS AND
CROWDED SCHEDULES

A NABEL: Honey, this next point is one of my favorite phrases from all of our materials concerning how Christ loves His Bride:

5. He Dedicated Himself to Her
That She Might Be Pure

And He also covered over all her imperfections with His love. Husband, we can accept something less than the perfect. How about this: *Please don't continually point out my mistakes to me.*

BILL: Colossians 3:19 reads as follows: "Husbands, love your wives, and do not be harsh with them" (RSV). It isn't cricket to hit your wife (though I sadly acknowledge that many husbands do), so we lash out at them with harsh words. The old adage, "Sticks and stones may break my bones but words will never harm me," simply is not true. If the inflictions made by thoughtless and cruel remarks from husbands were *visible* on their wives, then we would see gaping, bloody, festering wounds which never have the opportunity to heal. This obviously applies as well to wives who are critical of their husbands. Not one of us is impervious to the pain of verbal abuse.

ANABEL: I had taken some materials to a little Mom and Pop print shop in Missouri, and they were to be done on the following Thursday afternoon. On Wednesday, I was in the neighborhood, and I thought I'd stop by and see if they were ready. The wife wasn't quite sure: "Just a minute, Anabel, and let me check with my husband." Apparently, he didn't know (or didn't care) that his voice would carry over the pressroom noise to the front of the shop, because when she asked him about my materials, he let her know in no uncertain terms that the printing was not ready and that "any dummy" should have known that! And once he had started chewing her out, he decided to do a real good job of it and threw in a few more choice words.

I heard it all and felt terrible for having caused her such humiliation. She didn't come right back; she was doing what we wives who have suffered such treatment from our husbands call "regaining our composure." When she reappeared her mascara was smeared, and she was holding her bottom lip between her teeth.

Oh, Husband, please do not be harsh with me.

I was in the grocery store rushing around and had no intention of eavesdropping on the couple in front of me. I had noticed them earlier, and because of the way they were dressed, I don't believe the following interaction was due to a lack of funds in the grocery account. We were walking down the vegetable aisle. The woman was filling their basket; he was pushing it. She picked up a bunch of radishes and put them in the cart.

"Can't you tell those things are pithy? Put 'em back!" he barked.

She put them back. They went on down the aisle where she picked up a head of lettuce.

"Can't you read, woman? We don't need that stuff!"

She put the lettuce back. They went on to the bacon, and she put a couple of pounds into the basket. I won't tell you what he said then.

Oh, Husband, please don't be harsh with me.

Perhaps you will remember my telling you that I was valedictorian of my high school graduating class. I must confess to you that isn't as glorious as it sounds. There were only some sixty-four graduating students. Sigh.

I know a woman who was also valedictorian of her graduating class in California, but that was quite an honor in that there were over three thousand students in her high school. She married one of the outstanding young man in her class. And you say, "Well, that must have been a very successful marriage with two such fine people."

Let me remind you, that talented young woman had been patterned in the world system to be strong, a performer, a perfectionist, and super sensitive—just like me. But that young man had been patterned, too, to be strong, a leader, unchallenged and verbal. So very much like we were, Honey.

BILL: Yes, although I was never anyone's most-likely-to-succeed choice, I can identify with his being a threatened male and taking his frustrations out on his wife.

ANABEL: That woman today is not out giving seminars on victorious Christian living. She isn't in her home. She is in an institution, and that vocabulary that won her the coveted award of being valedictorian of her class has been reduced to two words . . . "yes" and "no."

I have known of her through mutual friends for years.

She came home for Christmas. She wanted so badly to be a part of the festivities. So she dressed (a major, laborious undertaking) and spent the day in the kitchen preparing Christmas dinner.

On Christmas evening, after all the preparations had been made, she sat down with her family to supper. She was wearing a lovely gown, and when something went amiss at the table, she moved to correct the wrong. As she did, her sleeve caught the glass of water at her side, spilling it across the table. Do you know what her husband said to her?

He said the same thing that he began saying to her in their first little honeymoon apartment. He had said it many different ways, but the message was always the same. He said it over and over and over until she finally believed him. At the dinner table that evening he said to her, "Can't you do anything right?"

Oh, Husband, please don't do this to me.

I am not emotionally equipped to handle such harshness. I realize that I frustrate you, and you get angry with me at times, but don't destroy me. You are to love me. Teach me. Be patient with me. Let your love cover all my imperfections. "Above all, keep fervent in your love for one another, because love covers a multitude of sins" (1 Peter 4:8).

BILL: Dear God, how grateful I am that You have so graciously shown me how to stop doing this to the dearest gift outside of Jesus that You've ever given me. How heartbreaking it would be to me, Jesus, if You treated the Church, as Your wife, like I treated mine for so long. Lord, show my brother, who is reading these words with such a hungry heart, that only by choosing to pick up the Cross and to let You live through him will he ever be able to experience victory over his flesh.

6. He Gave His Life for Her

BILL: Time is life on this planet. By simply *spending time* with my wife, I am able to *give my life* for her.

Anabel and I are people watchers. If you are a dentist, one of the first things you will notice about me is my teeth. That is your field of interest. If you're a hunter, you'll have a lot of bear stories to tell. Our field of interest is people and how they interact, so we watch people and tell people stories.

ANABEL: Dramas are enacted all around you; in fact, you may play a leading role in any number of one-act plays . . . .

All Smiles and Packages

ANABEL: The mall was rather crowded, folks shouldering bags, dragging children, walking arm in arm—all oblivious to the angry-looking man who sat stiff and nervous on the bench in front of Turnkey Records; his anger seethed at the passersby.

After a few moments his wife arrived, all smiles and packages. He stood up, enraged, and pointed to his watch.

"You were supposed to be back here five minutes ago! You could at least *try* to be on time. I expect you to be considerate of me. I didn't want to come in the first place; but oh no, you had to drag me on your damned shopping trip. And from the look of those packages, you've spent all of my money on your _____ _____ dresses! Let's go."

Spend time with me. . . .

Saturday Night Out

ANABEL: It was *the* Saturday night out on the town for them . . . a table for two in a quiet restaurant . . . flickering candles on a clean white cloth . . . enough to warm the heart of any wife. How she had anticipated this evening, doing her nails, hoping her hair would be just right for the occasion, fretting over what dress to wear so she might look her best for the date.

All in the world she wanted was to prolong every precious moment of this special evening out with the man she loved. She gave a little giggle, trying to make a light remark as she smiled at him and whispered, "Honey, don't eat so fast. You're going to be nearly finished before I even get my potato buttered." A bomb went off. Anyone within ten feet of them heard every word of his reply. "Well, if you think I'm going to sit here and dilly-dally around while you pick at your food until it gets cold, you've got another think coming! This was all your idea! I didn't want to come in the first place!"

Silence. He finished his steak, then ordered and ate his dessert. Without any further communication they left, half of her meal still there where she had picked at it after the explosion. It was a quiet little restaurant with flickering candles and clean white cloths on the tables.

Spend time with me. . . .

He Bought the Farm

BILL: Jane was fortyish, not the sort of woman who would turn every head, but an attractive lady nonetheless. She was having an affair and was planning to leave her husband and teenage sons as soon as her lover's divorce was final.

Jim, her husband, had been reared in extreme poverty. On one occasion things had been so bad that they had nothing in the house to eat but cornstarch. His mom had tried to make soup from it, but it was simply inedible. Jim vowed that he'd never be hungry again.

When Jane left him, Jim was working three jobs in an effort to pay off the farm which he insisted God had "led him to buy." He had not taken her out for dinner in over ten years. "We need to get our farm paid off," he kept telling her.

He frequently told his family that he was sacrific-
ing his all for them, but Jane and the boys just as
regularly told him they hated the farm with a passion
and had never wanted to move to the country in the
first place. His insensitivity caused Jane's sexual desire
to sink to zero until she finally ceased to respond to
his advances altogether.

It was at *this* point that Jim figured they had a
marriage problem and was motivated to solve it. He
decided that if Jane could get a job, the extra income
would enable them to clear the farm mortgage that
much sooner. This, he reasoned, would get her out of
the house more and relieve the pressure. She
obediently took a job as a waitress during the night
shift.

One rainy evening, a man came into the little
diner where Jane worked, took a seat in his regular
booth, and ordered a cup of coffee. He and Jane were
by themselves in the restaurant, and though she was
going about her duties, she was feeling lonely and
melancholy. He picked up on it.

"What's the matter, Jane? You seem down."

"Oh, no. I'm fine."

"Aw, come on. I can tell you aren't yourself."

"It would take all night for me to tell you my life
history. You don't have time for that."

"I'll *take* the time. Come on over and sit down. I'll
buy the coffee and you spill the problems. The boss
won't mind if you take a little break. Maybe I can
help."

And so she did . . . and he did. This was the man Jane was having the affair with . . . while Jim was paying off his farm.

Spend time with me. . . .

Crow's Nest

ANABEL: I still don't know just what the ingredients were that turned that rainy, blustery, chilly day in San Diego into such a lovely afternoon, but it *was* unforgettable. We had a layover, and instead of sitting in the airport, we took a city bus down to a village on the harbor. It was raining lightly, so we ran from store to store perusing the shelves. I bought some candles, and that was the extent of our purchases. We happened into a bookstore that had a loft where you could sit and have hot drinks and cookies. We browsed through the books, then took a cozy secluded table with a view of the bay and sipped our hot chocolate.

That's it. No thick, juicy steaks. No Hyatt Regency. No long-stemmed red roses. No surf. Just the two of us . . . together. Thanks, sweet husband. You made something that could have been tedious and boring very special by simply . . .

Spending time with me.

CONCLUSION

B ILL: Well, I'm sure you have some questions you're going to have to work through; that's to be expected. You probably have a good idea by now of just where the problems lie, and you know that the secret to living the Christian life is *not* discovered by way of rules, regulations, and concepts; rather, the Life of Christ *is* your life; He has *replaced* your old "lord-of-the-ring" life.

To experience Christ as Life requires a deep commitment. To step out, give up all control, and place yourself totally in His hands can be frightening. But the choice *is* yours. He will not impose His will upon you. He is totally committed to you, and you can either walk away or commit yourself totally to Him.

Would you like to pray together? Okay, let's join hands here in front of the fire. I'll pray and you repeat after me:

My Jesus,

I don't understand all of this completely (I doubt anyone does), but I believe that when You died at Calvary, I was in You and I died with You. When You were buried in that forsaken tomb, I, too, was buried; and when You were raised, I was re-created as a *new person* in You . . . I was born again.

There is only One who can live the Christian life — You — and I *now have Your Life.* I offer myself to You to express Your Life through me, and I want You to start in my own home with those You have given to me, with those who are most precious to me.

Jesus, I take my first step forward and rest in the certainty of You. Amen.

ANABEL: What a special time this has been for us. . . . Thanks for coming and letting us share with you.

BILL: Let's have supper together before too long. Remember, we love you . . . and we're praying for you. Goodbye.

ANABEL: Goodbye.

APPENDIX A

BIBLICAL PRIORITIES FOR A WIFE

A NABEL: Have you recognized the difference between the *revealed* will of God and the *impressed* will of God?

The *revealed* will of God is the *direct Word* of God. There are no questions about the revealed will of God. I don't "feel" anything; I don't put out a fleece; I don't ask Him thirty-six times if He is sure; I simply read it and then heed it. The revealed will of God is direct instruction—instruction that I am to place as my highest priority to accomplish.

We were *impressed* to move to Ft. Worth, Texas in 1981. There wasn't one single word in the Bible that told us where we were to go; no writing on the wall; no signs in the heavens. We "believed" that God was leading us to move from a very delightful environment, including home and friends, to a "foreign" country. That is the impressed will of God. Who you marry, the job you take, how much your offering should be for the visiting speaker, where you should go to school, etc.—all these decisions fall under the impressed will of God.

- Revealed Will: I *know* this is what God wants me to do from His Word.

- Impressed Will: I *believe* this is what God wants me to do.

Let me create a story in order to illustrate what I am saying. You have a family. Both you and your husband are very dedicated Christians. He is a pastor. You've just recently moved to this town. Your husband, and you yourself, "felt impressed" that this was the church that God wanted you to shepherd. You are walking in the "impressed" will of God. You have been obedient to that impression from Him and He is delighted. He will honor your trust and obedience.

But your husband is having to devote a great deal more time to his task than he had initially thought.

It's a larger church, and people pull at him from every direction. Committee meetings swallow up two nights a week, he has lunch nearly every day with one of the deacons, his counseling load escalates until he feels like he has the whole world on his shoulders, and the supper hour is taken by folks having you out to their house "just to get to know you."

You are neglected.

The children are neglected.

The "nest" is neglected.

Your husband is operating under the *impressed* will of God, but he is *not* operating under the *revealed* will of God.

Do you know what the *revealed* will of God is for your husband? It is not a nebulous revelation or an "I think" situation; rather, it is spelled out very carefully in the Scriptures. Number one is always number one: "Knowing God" (Philippians 3:10). But number two and number three are clearly *revealed* as well. Number two is to be a husband; number three is to be a dad. I believe if you will study this diligently *after the cross,* you will agree with this position.

Let's suppose that you say this to me: "I try not to bother my husband with household details or with problems that I feel like I can handle with the children. Goodness knows he has enough problems at work, and to come home and have to face more . . . well, I just protect him as much as I can. My needs seem so unimportant when you consider the things he has to deal with all day long.

Do you realize that in your zeal to "protect" your husband from family involvement you are allowing him to abort his God-ordained duty of walking in the revealed will of God? And when a person is out of God's *revealed* will, there *will be repercussions*. It could manifest itself in his personal life through a general restlessness, an emptiness, an obsession, or a compulsion to search for and capture something that is missing in his life. Or it could affect his relationship with his family, and he would not realize the estrangement until his children were grown and gone and his wife had built her life without him.

I've heard that story many times, only the job description changes. The husband may be a college professor, a church staff member, a doctor, an accountant, a businessman with heavy responsibilities, a man who works in unpleasant circumstances, or an engineer. It is not the job classification that matters; disordered priorities result in disordered lives.

There are three words that need to be understood if we are to realize our Biblical priorities:

1. *Volition:* the act of using the will; exercise of the will as in deciding what to do; a conscious or deliberate decision or choice

2. *Obligation:* to bind by a contract, promise, sense of duty

3. *Integrity:* incorruptibility; firm adherence to a code of moral values; quality or state of being complete or undivided.

Being obedient to the priorities set forth in the Scriptures is basic to obedience.

These are the Biblical priorities for a wife, using my situation as an illustration.

1. A personal relationship with Jesus

I am a beloved daughter — a cherished sister — a precious child — an unblemished bride — a member of God's family forever. I am to *know* Him.

2. A mate

As we have already elaborated in the husband/wife relationship, suffice it to say that I am the wife of Bill Gillham, a man of God. I am to edify him — become one with him.

3. A parent

I am the mother of Pres, Mace, Will, and Wade. I am to train them. I am to present the picture of a Godly woman to them, imprinting in their minds what they will seek in a mate. I am to make home a refuge, a haven, a place of security and safety. I am to become perceptually one with them, emotionally one with them, teaching them the elementary principles of physical oneness by touching and expressing love in acceptable ways . . . God's ways.

4. A member of an earthly family

I am Anabel HOYLE Gillham. I am to honor my mother and father, expressing my devotion to them, caring for them.

5. A person with gifts/talents

I am a counselor, lecturer, teacher called by God, gifted by God. I am to allow Him to minister through me with the gifts that He has given to me.

6. A friend

I am Anabel. A friend to some whom God has given especially to me. I am to love them, be sensitive to them, available to them when they need me.

7. A church member

I am a member of a very large family. Some of them are hurting. I am to minister to them. This is my church.

8. A witness to the world

I am to minister to a hurting world . . . a world redeemed by God through His beloved Son, spurned by millions. He will reach out through me to reveal Himself to this world.

I *volitionally* chose the first three priorities. One, I accepted God's plan—freely given; two, I chose a mate; three, I chose to bring children into the world by entering into the reproductive plan established by God.

Numbers four through eight have been given to me as a result of my volitional choice to accept and commit myself to Number One. I have, therefore, *obligated* myself to carry them out. I have entered into a covenant volitionally. *Integrity* is now the key word. Flawless integrity. Impeccable integrity.

If I live in the "lower priorities", omitting the "higher" ones, I am going to experience frustration. The Holy Spirit will exert pressure to guide me back into the proper order for my life. That pressure can range from mild to intense, but His purpose is pure.

As we stay within these God-ordained priorities, and as we love those He has given us and thus train them to love, the world will be drawn to the person of Jesus Christ . . . by our living witness.

APPENDIX B

TO BE TRULY FEMININE

A NABEL: One of the most tender and intimate moments I remember with my dad occurred while we were sitting out on the back-porch step one evening. I was sitting between his legs, and he had his arms around my neck. My mother had just undergone a hysterectomy. I didn't understand Dad's poignant words when he said to me, "You know, Honey, you're the only little boy I'll ever have."

I can't remember being a tomboy for my dad, but I was a super-duper tomboy. The neighborhood kids gathered in our backyard, and there were several boys in the group. That didn't matter to me. If we played cowboys and Indians, I was the chief. If we played cops and robbers, I was the head honcho — be it the sheriff or the "godfather." I even remember Dad tying ropes in the mulberry tree so I could be Tarzan.

Then there were the "races down under the hill" during recess in the sixth grade. I always won. Two grand defeats were Mervin McConnell and Joe Harold West. I reveled in defeating Joe Harold . . . he was my boyfriend.

Another "red-letter" day was the annual trek up Cavanal Mountain. I had a crush on Robert Henry Kendrick. How am I going to get him to notice me? Why, the same way I have been getting boys to notice me ever since the backyard get-togethers. I'll do whatever he does as well as he does — or better than he does. And I did. He was very definitely the leader of the pack, but I was right by his side all the way up to the top. I still can remember the thrill of sitting with him on the big flat rock looking out over the Poteau River Valley, waiting for the others to catch up with us. He noticed me! He said something to the effect of "You're quite a mountain climber." My heart fairly sang, but my joy was short-lived. He *carried* another little gal down the mountain because she had a blister on her foot! Sigh.

About this time, I became aware of something in the movies . . . Humphrey Bogart and Lauren Bacall. Nice. Then I saw *Mrs. Miniver* with Greer Garson and Walter Pidgeon. I liked what I saw. Two people — married — who had fun together, who respected each other as individuals, and who loved each other deeply. I began to think, "Maybe being a girl isn't all that bad."

Some people would call that "cultural conditioning." I call it "creationist conception." I was beginning to see what God had created me to be . . . something very beautiful . . . something very special . . . a female.

Femininity. What does it mean? If we asked a group of women that question, how many of their answers would reflect the culture of the day . . . career goals, the way we dress, the way we look, or possibly our understanding of personal fulfillment? Just how different would the answers be from those of a group of women in 1900, or in the Middle Ages, or in the time of Christ?

It is imperative that we have a standard — an immutable standard — if we truly want to discover the pure meaning of femininity.

The source of the word *feminine* is derived from the female, and the female was created by God. He said, "It isn't good for the man to be alone. I will create for him a helper to complete him" (Genesis 2:18, Amplified). Our understanding of "femininity" will come as we accept the impeccable integrity of God. He designed a "completer." Once we discover how the male is to be completed, then we can fulfill our feminine role by meeting the male needs.

How do I complete the male? It's certainly a great deal more than simply a sexual completion. As husband and wife (and Adam and Eve were husband and wife), we complete each other in *every aspect* of our beings.

But how? Consider the male's ability to gather data in a certain situation. Generally speaking, he is very logical, but he is not very intuitive. We, as females, are intuitive, so we add that dimension to his makeup. Or take, for instance, interpersonal relationships. The male is typically not as "people oriented" as we are. He is not emotionally designed like we are. Consequently, we add a depth of communication and sensitivity to him. Completing . . . feminine.

The male needs praise (Ephesians 5:33b, Amplified Bible). The female, being created to complete that need, should allow the male to perform for her so that she can praise him. That's part of being feminine. Should I refuse to meet that need, then I am negating my femininity. I am rebelling against God's plan.

The male needs headship (Ephesians 5:22). The female, being created to complete that need, can *allow* the male to operate as the head. That's being feminine. If I compete with the male for this role (be it my husband, my boss, or the meterman) by being domineering, aggressive, and demanding, then I am not "completing." I am denying my feminine makeup.

Like praise and headship, the male needs a physical relationship. This need is to be met within the bounds of God's rules; He created me and He knows what is best for His creation. Meeting this need is reserved for the marriage relationship. As I complete my husband physically, I am being feminine.

Rearing children is a uniquely feminine trait. That's part of being female. I was created physiologically to bear children. I have been given certain emotional qualities and certain intellectual qualities that are unique to the female and designed for the specific purpose of rearing my children. Yes, childbearing is definitely a part of the female role God lovingly bestowed upon me.

But, if completing the male and bearing and rearing children were all that I was created for as a woman, then there would be millions of unfulfilled women in the world today. Do you really think God is unaware of the desires that plague the single woman? Do you wonder if He knows the depth of despair that clouds the heart of the widow? To be needed—and have no one who needs me. To be given by God the innate desire to build a nest—and not have anyone to "feather the nest" for. Have you doubted that God knows the intensity of loneliness or the depth to which "yearning" reaches? Oh, yes. He knows. And He gave us answers long before there were our questions.

There are examples of women in the Bible that demonstrate that woman is of worth, not because of occupation, her status, or her accomplishments in the world system; rather, she is worthy simply because of who she is and because of the fruition of God's work in and through her.

Dorcas "abounded with deeds of kindness and charity" (Acts 9). She was a compassionate woman who met the needs of those around her.

Ruth's tenderness toward her bereaved mother-in-law was a declaration of true love and faithfulness (Ruth 1). She respected Naomi and obeyed her instructions.

Lydia was a businesswoman who sold "purple fabrics" (Acts 16). She opened her home to the early followers of Jesus and was a dedicated disciple.

Esther possessed great courage and discernment; it was her wisdom and boldness that saved the Jewish nation (Esther).

Mary, Martha's sister, was a woman of deep devotion. She took her costly perfume and bathed the feet of Jesus. "Oh, Mary, how foolish! How insignificant . . . as though He would notice." Oh, no. Her simple act of love for the Lord has been recorded so that we might realize how He desires our overt adoration (John 12:3).

Deborah was a judge of Israel, a national leader (Judges 4, 5). Mary was the mother of Jesus and a woman of great faith (Luke 2). The woman of Proverbs 31 was a well-organized and competent businesswoman. Rahab the harlot proved herself to be trustworthy and brave (Joshua 2, 6).

All this is feminine? Yes. I've listed as many different "job descriptions" as I have women. You cannot define femininity as something that a woman does. It must be defined as something that a woman *is*.

Every little girl comes into her world with the God-given need to be feminine. All females are created equal as far as these *innate* needs are concerned; however, each little girl's self-image *as a female* is molded by the people in her own unique world. Children, being self-centered, do not learn about other people in their world—they learn about *themselves* as people interact with them, touch them, communicate with them, and care for them. Because of this inherent self-centeredness, a little girl begins to learn about herself and her femininity from the first breath of earth-air she inhales.

If she could express her need, she might ask, "Why do I feel this way, Mother? Why did that make me cry? Why is my body different? Mother, teach me how to be feminine. What does it mean? Why am I special? How should I act?" If her mother does not heed her silent questions, then she will not learn positive things about herself; rather, she will come to doubt her femininity. This need lying deep within her will grow as she grows, but not into the facet of beauty that God intended. It will be deformed and intensify until it is completely out of proportion and eventually comes to control her.

Sexually promiscuous. Frigid. Fearful. Homosexual. Woman hater. Insecure. Deprived of love. Perverted. Introverted. Extroverted. Self-hate. The list of potential problems goes on and on describing the young woman who was never physically loved by her mother, whose mother never hugged her or kissed her or said to her, "I love you"; who never taught her feminine tasks or whispered choice feminine secrets; who never *affirmed* her daughter's femininity.

And then there's dad. "Carry me, Daddy. Let me go with you, Daddy. Can I hold your hand? How do I talk to men? Will they be as much fun as you are? Will I find someone just like you? You make me feel so special. Thank you, Daddy, for the talk last night."

"I love you, Honey."

"Yes, I know you love me, Dad."

And she delights in her femininity. But if she is deprived of her father's affection, she searches for "daddy's love" all through her life with an almost insatiable craving . . . to be held . . . to be touched . . . to be cherished . . . to be feminine.

But there is God. God created the female, and God can *re-create* the female as He tenderly fashioned her that day in the Garden. Oh, please listen. It isn't that you have been maimed and deformed beyond recognition—beyond hope. Oh, no. You are stained. You have been deceived. You have believed what people have *told* you—or you have suffered from what they have *not* told you. You have been deeply hurt by those who were intended to love you.

I wonder—do *you* understand what really happened when you came to Jesus and said to Him, "Oh, Jesus, Healer of all that is broken, please mold me and make me new"? He did just that; He took all of the unloveliness, the rejection, the broken heart—and made a new woman who is altogether lovely and totally accepted in His sight. Would you like to be someone different, someone who doesn't have to be controlled by what she has experienced in years past? You are, my dear one.

There is *nothing* that is impossible for God, nothing so ugly that He will turn His eyes away, so mutilated that it is beyond His ability to heal. He will take what the world has soiled and trodden under foot, and He will make it new. He will take the wounds so cruelly inflicted, and He will cleanse them with compassionate care. He whispers words of love and encouragement and will never release His firm grip on your hand. But you must ask Him to do these things. He does not force His will upon you and insist that you love Him. He patiently waits for you to accept all that He has done for you.

Therefore, if any *woman* is in Christ Jesus, she is a beautiful new creature. All of the old things that she learned about herself that were so destructive and hurtful have passed away. Look closely . . . you are *new* (see 2 Corinthians 5:17).

APPENDIX C

TO BE TRULY MASCULINE

You'll recall from my sharing about my flesh patterns in this book that I had a long struggle with striving to prove my masculinity so that I could accept myself. Laboring under the *feeling* that I was inferior to the macho males (but longing to be like them), I struggled to *feel* like a "real male." My stuck feeler was controlling me.

Had you observed me during high school as I related to strong, assertive girls, you would have heard me cutting them down with my sarcastic tongue; their strength motivated me to prove I was stronger than they were. When relating to the average males, I held my own fairly well; however, when a conflict occurred with the John Wayne types, you would have seen me passively accommodating them. Confrontation with a powerful male was always a severe setback in my effort to gain self-acceptance, and those times when they put me in my place in the pecking order were painful because I interpreted those experiences as hard evidence that I was less than a real male. To me, masculinity was defined as power . . . the power to outwit, to out-perform, to dominate any person who tried to overpower me; and because I could not consistently accomplish this, I felt like a failure.

My favorite movie plots involved an easygoing hero who patiently allowed the town toughs to push him around until he'd finally had enough; then, with either fists or guns, he'd wipe them out to the utter amazement of all. I think Deputy Barney Fife of the Andy Griffith Show would also probably go see those movies two or three times.

Often a boy is not affirmed in being male (ideally, by his dad) during his formative years. To affirm means: "To make firm; to declare positively; to assert; to confirm; to ratify; to validate."

The following are some ways a dad should affirm his son: He should spend time teaching his son masculine activities and interests (anything from mowing the lawn to talking about why geese migrate); he should wrestle with him, complete with grunts and groans in the "agony of defeat" when he lets his son win; he should take a genuine interest in the things in which his son is interested (be it the piano, athletics, stamp collecting or fishing). He should demonstrate physical love to him, allow his son to see warm looks of approval in his dad's eyes.

Experiences like these communicate, "I like you. You are a male like me. You are of very high value to me, and I'm proud to be your dad." At special times he should put a hand on his shoulder and say such things as, "I thank God for the day He brought you into my life. You are a fine guy, and I am proud you're my son." These kinds of things affirm a son in being a male and in being accepted as male.

If a son does not get this affirmation, he *does not learn* that his *dad* is falling down on the job; *he learns about himself*. He learns, "I am not very male. Therefore, I can't love myself. I could if I were really masculine. I wish I were masculine so I could respect myself, but I'm just not." As he matures, he usually manifests some sort of masculinity maladjustment ranging from over-passivity to over-dominance, from homosexuality to an insatiable heterosexual appetite, from a massive drive to succeed to feeling unworthy of success should it come, from being too introverted to extremely extroverted, *ad infinitum.*

A son's lack of affirmation as male can also be the result of having a domineering mother. Since God created a boy to become the loving leader of a wife and family someday, the boy needs to *perceive* himself as progressing toward that goal of maturity. But if his mom (the primary female with whom he relates in his formative years) is mega-strong and aggressive, then he's intimidated and *feels* it's a monumental, if not impossible, task to attain a level of leadership in the family. The emotional result will be what I emphasized in the previous paragraph.

With the escalation of the world's rejection of God's truth and subsequent acceptance of the feminist movement (even by many Christians), this problem is now rampant among young males. One can readily see the devastating effect that today's epidemic of divorce will have upon an entire future generation of young males. Many boys are not only being reared by strong, aggressive mothers, but they also have no father figures to affirm them *as* males; consequently, they constantly struggle to affirm *themselves* as male. I believe the subsequent frustration is the primary dynamic behind the rapid rise in homosexuality, rape, and wife abuse. This is especially evident among subcultures that are matriarchal in their family structure.

Some sons give up hope of being a *real* male. Something snaps, and with a lot of help from Satan, the boy, *longing for the male acceptance which he cannot bestow upon himself*, opts for homosexuality. Other boys partially give up hope of ever being a *real* male and become passive toward all power figures, both male and female. They seek security through weakness. Still others overtly rebel against their mother's dominance, reject their dad (who weakly submits to his wife's power), and build a macho facade to compensate for their *feelings* of inadequacy.

These facades become identities of their own making as they play "lord of the ring" and attempt to attain self-acceptance. Those of us who have traveled this road must not blame our folks. "For our struggle is not against flesh and blood, but against the rulers, against the powers, against the world forces of this darkness . . ." (Ephesians 6:12). We structured our own flesh patterns, and now we must let Christ liberate us from being controlled by them.

So how are we liberated? First, who infused masculine needs and traits into the male? God. The problem is that we have patterned ourselves after earthly male role models. You have either sought power over others or have given up and become passive. To solve your problem, you must first repent, then appropriate your new identity in Christ and begin to live as the man you *now* are.

Second, God is Spirit (see John 4:24), and He created us in His image; We are, therefore, spirit-beings. You must think of yourself as a male spirit-creature in an earthsuit, not as a male physical-creature with a spirit. God is your spiritual Father (see Hebrews 12:9).

Third, when you came to Christ, you were crucified (see Romans 6:6). You were then reborn as a new spirit-being in Christ and are no longer identified according to your flesh (see 2 Corinthians 5:14-17). In the Second Adam's lineage (see 1 Corinthians 15:45-48), you have a new present, a new future, and a new past. Your old macho, passive or homosexual ways are NOT YOU now! They are your old ways (which the Bible calls "flesh"), and now "we recognize no man according to the flesh" (2 Corinthians 5:16). You must set your mind on this truth . . . it is REALITY.

Fourth, what is a real male? *Where can we males find the ideal male role model?* Is it John Wayne? Mike Tyson? John Elway? Lee Iacocca? With due respect to these men, the answer is no. Who is the only perfect male who ever lived? The Male who was and is in all ways perfect; the One who inferred He is also the perfect Father figure by saying, "If you have seen Me, you have seen the Father." Yes, it's Jesus. You must now adopt this perfect masculine role model instead of the imperfect ones (even Dad) that you have emulated striving for self-acceptance as a male.

I state, with all reverence to the "real" Christ, that we have received the false impression from artists that Jesus was effeminate. Paintings which depict Him as spending more time at the hairdresser than in His workshop cannot be true. The God-man Jesus was a carpenter. They portray Him as if He couldn't even lift a hammer, let alone swing one all day. Even so, the case for Jesus' being the ideal male does not rest with the muscle tone of His earthsuit, but with His character and integrity. It matters not if His earthsuit was 5'2" or 6'2", if it was black, brown, red or white . . . that is important to carnal man, but not to God. He creates males and installs them in various-colored earthsuits sizes S to XL, and every inhabitant is capable of maturing into a real man.

Jesus was truly masculine. I do not speak of His power to walk on water or turn it into wine. I speak of His power to perform acts of *agape*. He lived completely in the definition of *agape*: "I will do the most constructive, edifying, redemptive thing I can do for you." He forgave people who burned Him. That's power. He rescued a humiliated woman who was about to be killed by the city fathers, knowing He'd lose credibility with some of them. That's power. He risked rejection from dear friends by confronting them. That's power. He lived for the best of others, not self. That's power. He passed up the chance to say, "I told you so," to Peter and fried him a fish dinner instead. That's power. He suffered an agonizing death (though innocent) and never begged His tormentors for mercy or for a plea-bargain. He even credited them for being blind to what they were doing. That's awesome power!

True masculinity is to be powerful, but for what purpose? To *obey* God. Letting Christ live through you by faith (that's power) produces love, compassion, gentleness (when required), firm confrontation (when required), patience, kindness, goodness, and integrity. It means to live a life of service, not survival. That's true Christ-like masculinity as modeled by the God who made you male and set Jesus before you as an example. It is God's goal to conform you to Christ's image (see Romans 8:29).

As the new man you now are, you're fully equipped to "life out" all the above characteristics of true masculinity through the indwelling life of Christ. He will do it for you. Yes, you will fail at times, but when you fail, confess it, thank God you're forgiven, and begin again.

So, lift up your head, new male in Christ. Begin each day by affirming yourself in your mirror as the "real" man you are RIGHT NOW (even if your earthsuit looks like it needs ironing). Allow Christ to live through you this day and begin to *agape* those in your own house. In so doing, you will grow into a mature male. You *are* affirmed in your masculinity by your True Father. You are *His* son (see John 1:12), and He is proud of you just because you're *His*. Feel His arm around your shoulders. Hear Him say to you, "You are Mine, and I am proud that you bear My Name. Today I desire to express My life through you to do My will on earth. Now, let's go *agape* 'em, son."

BIBLIOGRAPHY

Audio Tape Albums

Gillham, Bill, and Anabel Gillham. "Victorious Christian Living Seminar." Gillham Ministries, Inc., 1981. (Price: $29.95 P.P. This package includes a diagram booklet and eight and one half hours of teaching on how to apply the truths taught in *Marriage Takes More Than Two* to your marriage.)

Gillham, Bill, Preston Gillham, and Anabel Gillham. "Advanced Seminar on Victorious Christian Living." Gillham Ministries, Inc., 1985. (Price: $29.95 P.P. This package includes a diagram booklet and nine hours of additional teaching on applying the truths taught in *Marriage Takes More Than Two*. Also includes further emphasis on marriage application.)

Video Seminars

Gillham, Bill, and Anabel Gillham. "Victorious Christian Living." Gillham Ministries, Inc., 1984. (Price: $350.00 plus $5.00 UPS. This package includes eleven video cassettes [50-57 minutes each] dealing with the truths taught in *Marriage Takes More Than Two* and how to apply them to a marriage. It also includes a 55 page Leader's Discussion Guide. The 40 page viewers Study Guide is available for $2.50 each. Excellent for churches or home cell groups.)

Gillham, Bill, Anabel Gillham, and Preston Gillham. "Advanced Seminar on Victorious Christian Living." Gillham Ministries, Inc., 1986. (Price: $350.00 plus $5.00 UPS. This package includes ten video cassettes [50-53 minutes each] and covers additional teaching on how to apply the truths taught in *Marriage Takes More Than Two*. Also includes a further emphasis on marriage application.)

Any two video sets may be ordered for $600.00 plus $10.00 UPS.

Free fourteen minute promo of the "Victorious Christian Living Seminar" is available upon request.

Inquiries and orders may be sent to:

Gillham Ministries, Inc.
4100 International Plaza, Suite 520
Fort Worth, Texas 76109
Phone: (817) 737-6688

If you would like to receive Gillham Ministries' free monthly discipleship paper containing articles on the believer's true identity in Christ along with the Gillhams speaking schedule, please send your printed address to the address given above.